LIVING
in the
REVELATION
of
JESUS CHRIST

Elaine W. Hart

ISBN 978-1-0980-7616-0 (paperback)
ISBN 978-1-0980-7617-7 (digital)

Christian Faith Publishing, Inc.
832 Park Avenue
Meadville, PA 16335
www.christianfaithpublishing.com

Printed in the United States of America

CHAPTER 1

Revelation 1:1–20

Dear children, this is the last hour, and as you have heard,
the Antichrist is coming. Even now, many antichrists
have come. This is how we know it is the last hour.

—1 John 2:18–19

REVELATION 1:1–8. This is a vision of events
in the future, revealed by Jesus Christ to His servant John. An angel explains the vision's meaning, and John writes down the Words of God and
of Jesus Christ. If you read this prophecy aloud
you will be blessed. If you listen and heed what
it says you will also be blessed. The time is near
when these things will all come true. Grace and
peace to the seven Churches in Asia from Jesus
Christ who loves us and has freed us from our
sins by His blood. He is coming in the clouds
and everyone will see Him. He says, "I Am the
Alpha and the Omega, the Almighty. I was, I
Am, I will come."

Some two thousand years ago, God sent His Son, Jesus Christ, to
make this revelation to us through His apostle John. John was
in exile on the Isle of Patmos at that time because he witnessed for
the Lord. He was probably near the age of ninety at that time. Jesus

wanted us, His followers, to know what was going to take place. John wrote it all down. We are promised that if we read this aloud to the church, we will be blessed, and if we heed this warning, we will be blessed, because every day we are closer to fulfillment of this prophecy.

John the Baptist introduced John to Jesus (John 1:35–40). According to the apostle John himself, he was the "disciple Jesus loved" (John 13:23–24). John must have had a temper, because Mark tells us that Jesus called him "Son of thunder" (Mark 3:17). John was a businessman. His family were fisherman on the Sea of Galilee, and John sold their product in Jerusalem. The Jewish priests were customers, and John knew his way around the temple compound. That is why he was able to observe the proceedings after the arrest of Jesus, when Peter had to remain at the gate (John 18:12–17). From the cross, Jesus entrusted John with the care of His mother, Mary (John 19:25–27).

John and his brother James asked Jesus for the honor of sitting at His right hand and His left hand when He came into His kingdom. Jesus asked if they could of drink His cup and be baptized with His baptism. Jesus told them that, indeed, they would drink of His cup (Mark 10:35–40). This is why we believe that both were martyred. James was the first apostle martyred at the hand of King Herod (Acts 12:1–2). It is believed that John, who at about the age of one hundred, became the final martyred apostle. John survived exile on Patmos and returned to Ephesus, where it is believed he died near the turn of the second century. Eusebius called John a "martyr" (Eusebius, The Church History, 5:24).

He was imprisoned, but he wrote the message down because he knew that somehow the Lord would get it to us. After all, some six hundred years earlier, God had delivered the writings of the prophet Jeremiah (who had been carried all the way down to Egypt after the fall of Jerusalem) to Daniel (who was in exile all the way up in Babylon).

> This land shall become a wasteland. Israel and
> her neighbors shall serve the King of Babylon for
> 70 years. When these years of slavery are ended,
> I will punish the Babylonians for their sins.
> (Jeremiah 25:11–12)

> It was in the first year of the reign of Darius, son
> of Xerxes, that I, Daniel, learned from the Word
> of the Lord given to Jeremiah the Prophet, that
> Jerusalem must lie desolate for 70 years. I ear-
> nestly pleaded with the Lord in sackcloth and
> ashes. (Daniel 9:1–4)

The Lord wanted Daniel to read Jeremiah's writings. The Lord also wants us to read the writings of His messenger John. God has always had a plan, and He has shared His plan with His people down through the ages. So toward the end of the exile of the Israelites in Babylon, the Lord sent the angel Gabriel to reveal to Daniel the coming ages, all the way to eternity.

The children of Israel were in Babylon because they had rebelled against God and His ways for so long and so consistently that God had allowed the Babylonians to destroy Jerusalem and the temple and to carry them away. God had expressed through His prophet Hosea the thought that Israel was God's unfaithful wife, that God loved Israel, and that Israel would eventually return to Him.

> I will punish her for the incense she burned to
> Baal, and for the times she went looking for lov-
> ers and deserted Me. But I will court her again
> and bring her back to the wilderness and speak
> tenderly to her. I will return her vineyards and
> she will respond and sing with joy. In that com-
> ing day, she will call me "Husband" instead of
> "Master." O Israel, I will cause you to forget your
> idols. (Hosea 2:13–17)

The exile of the Judeans began in 605 BC, when Jerusalem was invaded by Babylon (Iraq), and Nebuchadnezzar carried the first group of captives, including Daniel, to Babylon (Daniel 1:1–4). However, the complete exile into Babylon took a few years. The Judeans were first called "Jews" in Babylon. However, members of all the tribes were preserved. Also, 605 BC began the time of the

Gentiles when the land was enjoying its rest. We are still in the time of the Gentiles.

Then, after seventy years in exile, they were allowed to return to the land. Israel was again a nation preparing for the birth and death of the Messiah, Jesus Christ. However, Israel has never since been the center of the world.

As soon as the Messiah was delivered and had offered the Perfect Sacrifice for our sins, Israel was again overcome, this time by Daniel's third empire. The Roman Empire destroyed Jerusalem and the temple in AD 70, some forty years after the death and resurrection of Jesus. God's plan is still His plan playing out over the ages (Revelation 12:1–6).

> Who has ever heard of such a strange thing?
> In one day the Nation Israel shall be born. In
> a moment as the pains begin, the baby is born.
> (Isaiah 66:8)

Suddenly, almost two thousand years after the destruction of Jerusalem, on May 14, 1948, Israel again became a nation—in one day! We know that this was always God's plan, because God had whispered this to His prophet Isaiah some 2,600 years before it happened. Now God has again brought her "back to the wilderness."

God's plan continues to move forward. With the return of Israel, God's wife, into the land, we stand on the verge of entering the seventieth week revealed to Daniel. Prophecy has been fulfilled, but there is not a temple in Jerusalem. Will that temple be built prior to entering the seventieth week, or will the temple be built at the beginning of the final week after the prince "makes a covenant with many"? Is the prince alive today?

Notice all the sevens. In the Bible, seven is the number of completion.

Seventy weeks. Daniel 9; Daniel 12. Daniel lived through the entire exile and beyond. When Daniel read in Jeremiah's writings that Israel would be in exile for seventy years, he knew that they had served their time, and he earnestly prayed that God would permit their return to the land. In answer God sent His angel Gabriel to reveal to Daniel that God's plan will play out in seventy "weeks," with a significant, important interruption. These "weeks" are actually years, not days. Thus, a "week" is a period of seven years.

> Seventy weeks are decreed for your people and for the Holy City to end their transgression, to reconcile with God and bring in everlasting righteousness, to complete this prophecy, and to anoint the Most Holy. Understand: From the issuing of the command to restore Jerusalem until the Messiah shall be 7 weeks and 62 weeks. The streets and the wall shall be rebuilt in troublesome times. After 62 weeks the Messiah shall be cut off.

> The prince who is to come will destroy the City and the Temple; the end will come like a flood. War will continue until the end of the determined desolation. The prince shall make a covenant with many for 1 week. In the middle of the week he shall bring an end to sacrifice and offering. On a wing of the Temple he will set up an abomination which causes desolation until the decreed end is poured out on him. (Daniel 9:24–27)

Seven weeks. The first seven weeks (forty-nine years) began in 445 BC, after the Babylonian Empire fell to the Persian Empire and King Cyrus of Persia (Iran) issued the order for the Israelites to rebuild the temple at Jerusalem (Ezra 1:1–4).

(As an interesting aside: Xerxes I, a.k.a. Ahasuerus, who reigned in Persia 485–465 BC, was the husband of Queen Esther. It is not known whether Esther was the mother of his successor, Artaxerxes I. Did God influence the impending events through Esther's presence in the palace?)

Sixty-two weeks. The next sixty-two weeks (434 years) began in 397 BC, When King Artaxerxes allowed Nehemiah to return to rebuild the city of Jerusalem (Nehemiah 1:1–2:8). These sixty-two weeks lasted until AD 37, after the crucifixion and resurrection of the Messiah, Jesus Christ. He was "cut off," but He was not destroyed. Jesus has continued His guidance from heaven.

We are living in the two-thousand-year interval between the end of the sixty-two weeks and the future onset of the final one week. This interval is known as the church age, which will end with the Rapture. (We are also still in the time of the Gentiles, which will continue until the return of Jesus Christ.)

One week. The final week (seven years) of God's plan will kick off with fulfillment of Rosh Hashanah—the Rapture of the church (Leviticus 23:23–25; 1 Thessalonians 4:15–17). This will end the church age, because Christians will move to heaven to be with their Lord. The rest of the world, including Israel, will be in the hands of "the prince" (the Antichrist) who will be allowed to take control (Revelation 6:2).

The time of the Gentiles began when God allowed the Babylonian Empire to conquer Israel. While Babylon was a young empire, God revealed the ensuing empires to Nebuchadnezzar and Daniel. These empires have held power on Earth for some 2,600 years.

The empires: Daniel 2; Daniel 7. The Lord revealed to His prophet Daniel the empires that would rule the world until the end of time. His first revelation of this to Daniel was initiated by a dream that came to Nebuchadnezzar, king of Babylon. Nebuchadnezzar was greatly disturbed by the dream, but, incredibly, he could not even remember the dream. God revealed the dream and its meaning to Daniel so that Daniel could inform Nebuchadnezzar.

> O King, in your dream you saw a huge, frighten-
> ing statue of a man. The head was made of pure
> gold, and its chest and arms were made of sil-
> ver. The statue's belly and thighs were formed of
> brass, and his legs were made of iron. The feet of

the statue were mixed iron and clay. God hurled
a Rock which crushed the feet of iron and clay,
and then the statue collapsed into pieces so small
that the wind blew them away. The Rock became
a great mountain that covered the Earth. (Daniel
2:31–35)

Babylon. Daniel then explained the meaning of the dream to
Nebuchadnezzar. Babylon (Iraq) was the golden head—the first
empire of the Time of the Gentiles. Babylon was represented as a lion
in God's later revelation of the empires to Daniel himself (Daniel
7:4). Daniel explained that God had given Nebuchadnezzar his position as king of the first great empire. The empire lasted only about
76 years, only long enough to accomplish the 70 years of the exile
of Israel.

Persia. Persia (Iran) was the second great empire. Persia was
the silver arms and chest of the statue revealed to Nebuchadnezzar.
Persia was represented as a bear in God's revelation of the empires to
Daniel personally (Daniel 7:5). Around 700 BC, long before Cyrus
was born, God had spoken of this future king of Persia through the
prophet Isaiah, even called him by name. Then, some 160 years
later, one night in October 539 BC, Persia invaded and overcame
Babylon in one night while Nebuchadnezzar's heir was indulging in
a drunken party. God had commended Cyrus for his future actions,
which would allow the Israelites to return to their Land.

> When I say, "Cyrus is My shepherd," he will obey,
> and Jerusalem will be rebuilt and the Temple will
> be restored. I have spoken it. (Isaiah 44:28)

Cyrus, the Persian king, did obey God around 519 BC.

> I, Cyrus, King of Persia, announce that Jehovah
> the God of Heaven has given me all the king-
> doms of the world. He has appointed me to
> build a Temple for Him in Jerusalem, in the

> Land of Judah. All Jews throughout the king-
> dom may now return to Jerusalem to rebuild this
> Temple to Jehovah, who is the God of Israel and
> of Jerusalem. May His blessings rest upon you.
> (Ezra 1:2–3)

Cyrus sent the temple furnishings which had been taken
to Babylon (Ezra 1:5–11). He allowed more than fifty thousand
Israelites to return home to rebuild the temple (Ezra 2:1–70). The
temple was rebuilt, but the rebuilding of the city of Jerusalem did not
begin until 445 BC. Artaxerxes I of Persia commissioned Nehemiah
to rebuild the city. These dates are important, because they are part of
Daniel's seventy weeks (Daniel 9:20–27). The commission to rebuild
Jerusalem in 445 BC (Nehemiah 2:1–9) began the sixty-two weeks
of Daniel's prophecy—the countdown to the Messiah!

Greece. The third great empire was Greece. Greece was represented in Nebuchadnezzar's dream as the statue's brass thighs (Daniel
2:31–35), and it was represented as a leopard with four heads in God's
revelation of the empires to Daniel (Daniel 7:6). Alexander the Great
conquered Persia in 331 BC, but he only reigned from 331–323 BC.
In 332 BC, Alexander visited Jerusalem. He was welcomed by the
Israelites, who told him that he was spoken of by the prophet Daniel.
Upon Alexander's death, the Greek Empire was divided among his
four generals—the leopard's four heads.

Rome. Rome was the fourth great empire. It was revealed in
Nebuchadnezzar's dream as the statue's legs of iron (Daniel 2:33).
In God's revelation of the empires to Daniel, Rome is depicted as
an animal with ten horns and huge iron teeth (Daniel 7:7). Rome
ended the nation of Israel in AD 70 when Titus destroyed Jerusalem
and the temple.

The Roman Empire continued through coalitions down
through the ages. In AD 330, the emperor Constantine moved the
seat of the Roman Empire to Constantinople where it remained until
AD 1453, when Constantinople was overcome by the Ottomans.
The Vatican remained in Rome until AD 1309, when it was moved

to France. It remained in France for almost seventy years and then returned to Rome in AD 1377.

New Roman Empire. While Daniel watched, he saw another empire growing out of the remnants of the Roman Empire. Daniel sees it as a small horn growing out of and then uprooting three of the original horns (Daniel 7:8). The little horn boasts and speaks against God. It makes war against the saints.

The Roman Empire never really ceased to exist. It was not conquered; it just lingered. We have now entered the fifth empire of Nebuchadnezzar's dream—the feet of iron and clay. The European Union, which came into existence November 1, 1993, is the New Roman Empire. The European Union adopted a flag of hyacinth blue with a circle of twelve gold stars (Revelation 9:17). Its parliament located in Strasbourg, France, is designed to resemble the Tower of Babel. The little horn will be the antichrist who will rule for Daniel's final seven years. We may already be seeing the first horn uprooted: Brexit (Revelation 13:1:5–8).

The rock. God revealed to Daniel the second coming of Jesus Christ (Daniel 7:1–14). Jesus Christ is the Rock. He will destroy the prince (the antichrist), and He will establish His millennial kingdom at the end of Daniel's seventieth week. The antichrist and the false prophet will be thrown into the lake of fire (Revelation 19:11–21).

The second coming of Jesus Christ will occur at the end of Daniel's seventieth week. Paul told us about this event.

> To those who are suffering, God will give you rest when Jesus appears suddenly from Heaven in flames, with His mighty angels. He will bring judgment on those who refuse to accept salvation through Jesus Christ. They will be separated from the Lord forever, never to see His glory and power. (2 Thessalonians 1:8–10)

We have been living in the time of the Gentiles since 605 BC when the first Israelites were conquered and carried to Babylon. We have been living in the Christian era since the death of Jesus Christ.

The Christian era will end with the Rapture (1 Thessalonians 4:16–17). The time of the Gentiles will continue until the second coming of Jesus Christ (2 Thessalonians 1:7–10). The second coming of Jesus Christ will occur seven years after the Rapture, at the end of Daniel's seventieth week.

> Then I will appear in the sky and the Nations of the Earth will mourn. They will see the Son of Man coming on the clouds with power and glory. (Matthew 24:30)

Today, in our time, God has brought Israel "back to the wilderness" (Hosea 2:14). Israel is back in the land. Possibly the only thing which is holding up the onset of Daniel's seventieth week is the rebuilding of the temple. However, that may not be holding things up. The antichrist will enter into an agreement with Israel at the beginning of Daniel's seventieth week (Daniel 9:27), and the temple may be rebuilt under that agreement.

We know that a temple will exist at the end of the first three and a half years of that agreement, because the Antichrist will desecrate it with an "abomination which causes desolation" (Daniel 11:31). Could this be the false prophet's statue of the antichrist (Revelation 13:14–15)? There is precedent. In 168 BC, during the period between the Old Testament and the New Testament, a Syrian, Antiochus Epiphanes, set up a statue of Jupiter in the holy of holies of the temple. Jesus Himself told us that Antiochus Epiphanes's prior desecration of the temple in 168 BC had not fulfilled Daniel's prophecy. This despicable act will be repeated in the middle of the seventieth week of Daniel's prophecy. Jesus described this future event, saying,

> When you see the abomination which causes desolation spoken of by Daniel the Prophet standing in the Holy Place, then those in Judea must flee into the mountains. (Matthew 24:15)

The final three and a half years of Daniel's seventieth week will be the worst that mankind has ever known. The Israelites will flee, and God will shelter His wife in a place He has prepared for her (Revelation 12:6). Some people speculate that Jordan (Edom) may be the safe place. They speculate that God will shelter the Israelites at Petra, in Jordan. Isaiah gives us a hint that this may be true. When Christ returns to begin His millennial reign, Isaiah tells us that He will come from the direction of Jordan. Will His first stop be to reveal Himself to the children of Israel? Will this be when the Day of Atonement—Yom Kippur—will be fulfilled (Leviticus 23:26–32). Will this be when Israel will "see the One they pierced and mourn for Him as for an only son" (Zechariah 12:10)?

> Who is this coming from Edom, from Bozrah, with crimson stained garments? Who is this in splendid robes striding forward in the greatness of His strength? (Isaiah 63:1)

> REVELATION 1:9–20. While worshiping the Lord on a Sunday, the Lord's Day, exiled on the Island of Patmos for preaching the Word, I suddenly hear the Voice of a Trumpet say, "Write on a scroll everything you see and send letters to the seven churches of Asia: Ephesus, Smyrna, Pergamos, Thyatira, Sardis, Philadelphia, and Laodicea. I, John, turn to see who is speaking. I see seven golden lampstands, and Jesus is standing among them dressed in a long robe with a golden waistband. His hair is snow white, and His eyes are like fire. His feet are like polished bronze, and His face is like the sunshine. He holds seven stars in His right hand, and a sharp, double-edged sword comes from His mouth. I fall at His feet. "Do not be afraid. I was dead, but I Am alive forever. I hold the keys to Death and Hades. The seven lampstands are the seven

> Churches of Asia, and the seven stars are the
> Angels of those Churches."

We know that the sword coming from His mouth is the Word of God.

> The Word of God is living and powerful and
> sharper than a double-edged sword. It penetrates
> to the soul and spirit, and it judges the intents of
> the heart. (Hebrews 4:12)

John must recognize his friend, Jesus, even though He looks so different. Jesus said the golden lampstands, or menorah, were the seven churches of Asia. Zechariah described the menorah.

> Then the angel who had been talking with me
> asked, "What do you see? I answered, "I see a
> golden lampstand holding seven lamps. At the top
> is a reservoir for the olive oil which flows to the
> lamps through seven tubes." (Zechariah 4:1–2)

First, Jesus speaks to the seven churches of Asia. These churches were the result of the missionary activities of Paul and the apostles, and then the dispersion of Christianity around AD 70 when Rome destroyed Jerusalem. The Lord had instructed His disciples to, "Go into all the world" (Mark 16:15) and when the Roman emperor Titus Caesar sacked Jerusalem and the temple in AD 70, everyone fled. Josephus told us the Romans spared a portion of the wall to serve as a garrison for the Roman soldiers. They left some towers so that posterity would know what a great city they had destroyed. The rest of the wall was leveled to the ground, and they even dug up the foundation. No one would even believe it was ever inhabited (Josephus, the Wars of the Jews 7:1.1).

Jesus speaks with the voice of a trumpet. Paul told us that when the time arrives to call Christians to heaven (the Rapture), Jesus will appear in the clouds and call us with the sound of a trumpet, and we will meet Him in heaven (1 Thessalonians 4:15–18). This impending event when Christ will call Christians to heaven with the sound of a trumpet is known as the Rapture. The Israelites have commemorated this future event by celebrating the Feast of Trumpets in September or October every year since God handed down Rosh Hashanah to Moses on Mount Sinai. The Rapture will come at the beginning of Daniel's seventieth week, just before the antichrist will be released to make war on the Earth (Revelation 6:1–2).

> The Lord instructed Moses, "On the first day of the seventh month you are to celebrate a day of complete rest and sacred assembly commemorated with the blowing of trumpets and a burnt offering." (Leviticus 23:23–25)

The second coming of Jesus, when He returns to establish His thousand-year reign, is a subsequent event, which will occur seven years after the Rapture, at the end of Daniel's seventieth week (2 Thessalonians 1:8–10).

CHAPTER 2

Revelation 2:1–20

If we die with Him, we will live with Him. If
we endure, we will reign with Him.
If we disown Him, He will disown us. If we
are unfaithful, He will remain faithful.
He cannot disown Himself.

—2 Timothy 2:11–13

Christ dictated to John letters to the angels of the seven churches of Asia. The seven stars which He held in his right hand represented these angels, and He held them close. These letters outline praise for the good lives that Christians were living and His criticism of and condemnation of the sins of those who were not living according to His teachings. These letters are important to us today, because the praise and the condemnation apply to us who represent Him here on Earth today. These same sins are rampant today. We backslide. We are sexually immoral. We worship the idols of money and power. As time grows shorter and shorter, and as Satan becomes desperate in these end-times, it is important for us each to "study to show ourselves approved by God" (2 Timothy 2:15). All these churches were in what is now Turkey. Today, the entire area is Muslim.

REVELATION 2:1–7. To the Angel of the Church at Ephesus: I hold the seven stars in My right hand and walk among the seven lampstands. I know that you work hard and have endured hardship. And you have not become weary. I know that you test insincere people who claim to be Apostles, and that you do not tolerate evil people, and share My hatred of the practices of the Nicolaitans. But you have lost the joy of your salvation, and no longer serve me with zeal. Recognize the height from which you have fallen. Repent and return to your first love, or I will remove your lampstand. If you have an ear, hear what the Spirit says to the Churches. If you overcome, I will give you the right to eat from the Tree of Life in God's Paradise.

Jesus encouraged the Ephesians to remember their original joy in their salvation, and to return to Him. If they continued to fall away, He would come quickly and remove their lampstand—in other words, the church was dying of lethargy. Jesus Christ promised that those who would listen to the Holy Spirit and come back to life would receive fruit from the tree of life in the New Jerusalem (Revelation 22:1–2).

Remember, the tree of life was in Eden. After Adam and Eve sinned by eating from the tree of knowledge of good and evil, God banished them from Eden so they could not eat from the tree of life and live forever (Genesis 3:22–24). Those who endure will eat from the tree of life.

The prophet Isaiah described God's people who had grown cold in their worship (Isaiah 6:9–10). Jesus quoted Isaiah.

You will hear but never understand; you will see but never perceive because your heart is calloused. Your ears hardly hear, and you have closed your eyes. Otherwise, you might see and hear, and understand, and I would heal you. (Matthew 13:14–15)

When Jesus wrote this letter, Ephesus was the fourth largest city in the Roman Empire. The church at Ephesus began under the preaching of Paul (Acts 19:1–12). Paul had visited Ephesus on his second missionary journey (Acts 18–19), and he spent two years at Ephesus on his third missionary journey. Ephesus was the center of the worship of Artemis, the Greek goddess of fertility. Worship of Artemis amounted to sexual orgies, and her followers had caused a riot against the Christians (Acts 19:23–41). Paul probably wrote the epistle to the Ephesians while in prison in Rome around AD 62. Following the Diaspora of AD 70, the apostle John, who wrote down this revelation of Jesus, and Mary the mother of Jesus lived out their lives at Ephesus. Today, a domed Catholic and Muslim shrine remains which is known as the "House of the Virgin Mary."

Ephesus today is a Muslim city named Selçuk, with a population of around eight hundred thousand people. The church died in the AD second century.

> REVELATION 2:8–11. To the Angel of the Church of Smyrna: I Am the First and the Last. I died and was resurrected. I know your works, and the tribulation which you have endured. I know your poverty, but you are rich in your salvation. I know how those who claim to be Jews but are a synagogue of Satan slander you. Satan will put some of you in prison and will persecute you to the point of death, but do not be afraid. If you have an ear, hear what the Holy Spirit says to the Churches. Be faithful and I will give you the Crown of Life and you will not face the second death.

James, the half brother of Jesus, counseled us to be faithful, and he spoke of the promise of the crown of life.

> Blessed are those who endure trials, for they will receive the Crown of Life which God has promised to those who love Him. (James 1:12)

Jesus was pleased with the Christians at Smyrna. He offered no criticism. The persecution of the Christians at Smyrna continued. The Bishop of the Church at Smyrna was John's friend Polycarp, who was burned at the stake in AD 155 for refusing to renounce Jesus. Jesus promised that those who did not renounce Him would receive the crown of life—they would not face the second death in the lake of fire (Revelation 20:11–15).

The city has been continuously inhabited, and today the city of three million people is known as Izmir. Izmir is officially Muslim, but it is a modern secular city, and some Christian churches are found there.

> REVELATION 2:12–17. To the Angel of the Church of Pergamos: I Am the sharp, two-edged sword. I know that Satan has set up his throne in your midst, but you are holding fast to My Name. You have not denied Me, even when Antipas was martyred. However, there are those among you who are sexually immoral, and some who are following the hated teachings of Balaam and of the Nicolaitans. You are eating food sacrificed to idols. If you do not repent, I will fight you with the Sword of the Word of God. If you have an ear, listen to what the Holy Spirit says to the Churches. If you overcome these sins, I will give you manna to eat, and a white stone with a new name engraved on it.

God prepared manna for the children of Israel during their forty-year journey in the Sinai Dessert. God called it "bread from heaven." It looked like coriander seeds and tasted like honey wafers. The Israelites gathered it every morning for forty years (Exodus 16:16–34). When they reached the promised land, the daily provision of manna ceased (Joshua 5:12).

David told us that manna is the food of angels!

> He opened the doors of heaven and manna
> rained down for them to eat. They ate the food
> of Angels! (Psalm 78:23–25)

Christ also promised that He would give a new name engraved
on a white stone to those who overcame; it was a Roman custom to
give such a stone to victorious athletes. Isaiah had also told the people that God would give them a new name: the bride.

> The nations shall be blinded by your righteousness, and God will give you a new name... Never
> again will you be called Desolate. Your new name
> will be The Bride, because the Lord will claim
> you as His own. (Isaiah 62:2–4)

Antipas was John's friend, and he was bishop of the Church of
Pergamos. He was martyred for refusing to offer sacrifices to idols. A
temple to the Greek god Zeus was located at Pergamos, and that is
probably why Jesus called it Satan's throne.

The modern-day town is named Bergama, with a Muslim population of around sixty thousand. It is known for production of fine
hand-woven carpets.

> REVELATION 2:18–29. To the Angel of the
> Church at Thyatira: I Am the Son of God. My
> eyes are like blazing fire, and My feet are like burnished bronze. I know your love and your faith. I
> know your service and diligence. But I also know
> that you have allowed that Jezebel, who calls
> herself a prophetess, to seduce My servants into
> sexual immorality, and to eat food sacrificed to
> idols. She is not repentant, so she and her followers will become ill. Those who do not repent, will
> suffer great tribulation and die. You will know
> that I search your minds and hearts and that you
> will receive according to your deeds. If you have

not listened to her teachings, I will not place any burden on you. Hold on to what you have until I come. Those who have an ear and hear what the Holy Spirit says to the Churches will receive the Morning Star and authority over the Nations.

Daniel also had seen the preincarnate Jesus and had described Him some six hundred years earlier.

As I was standing by the Tigris River, I looked up and saw a Man dressed in linen, with a belt of pure gold. His body was like chrysolite and His face was like lightning. His eyes were like flaming torches, and His arms and legs gleamed like polished bronze. His voice was like the sound of the multitude. (Daniel 10:4–6)

Apparently, there was a woman in their midst who was holding herself out as a follower of Christ while seducing the men, who were willing victims. God was going to take care of that situation—probably with gonorrhea (which was rampant in the first century).

Lucifer (Satan) was called the morning star until he rebelled against God, so that position is open (Isaiah 14:12–20). The morning star shines bright when the long night is ending and daybreak is imminent. Christians need to be shining brightly. The long night is ending. Daybreak is near.

Today Akhisar, a modern city of around one hundred thousand people, lies among the ruins of Thyatira. Its industries include the production of olives and textiles. There is no church, and there are no known Christians.

CHAPTER 3

Revelation 3:1–22

> Seek good and not evil so that you may live. The
> Lord will be with you as you say He is.

> —Amos 5:14

REVELATION 3:1–6. To the Angel of the Church of Sardis: I hold the seven Spirits of God, and the seven stars. I know your deeds. You are dead; wake up! Your deeds are not acceptable. Remember what you have received. Repent and obey what you have heard. If you do not wake up, I will come like a thief. But you do have a few who are not soiled. They are worthy and will wear white and walk with Me. If you overcome, you will be dressed in white and I will never remove your name from the Book of Life. If you have an ear, hear what the Holy Spirit says to the Churches, and I will acknowledge your name before My Father and His Angels.

There were a few who had not turned away from the Lord, and they were worthy. They would walk with Him, dressed in fine white linen (Revelation 19:8), and their names would be written in the Book of Life (Revelation 21:27). If those whose deeds were unacceptable would overcome their sin, they could also walk with Jesus dressed in white, and He would acknowledge them before His Father and His angels. If they did not wake up, He would come for them unannounced.

> Be prepared. You do not know what day your Lord is coming. If you knew when the thief was coming you would have kept watch. So you must be ready for My unannounced return." (Matthew 24:42–44)

Jesus did not mention worship of the goddess of the hunt, as the distraction of the Christians at Sardis, but she would certainly have been an attraction. Her temple was the fourth largest in the world, but today only a couple of columns remain. The Sardinians had been worshipping the Greek version of the goddess of the hunt and the moon, Artemis, for five hundred years. At the time Jesus Christ was walking on this Earth, the fourth empire—the Romans—were worshiping their goddess of the hunt, Diana, at Sardis.

They could not worship God and Diana. Jesus told us,

> You cannot serve two masters. You will hate one and love the other. You will despise one and be devoted to the other. You cannot serve God and mammon. (Matthew 6:24)

Today, the village of Sart, with a population of about five thousand people, remains. It is a farming community, and there are no known Christians in the area.

> REVELATION 3:7–13. To the Angel of the Church in Philadelphia: I Am holy and true. I hold the Key of David. What I open no one can close, and what I close no one can open. I know your deeds. No one can close the door to you. You are not strong, but you have kept My Word and have not denied Me. I will make those of

> the synagogue of Satan who say they are Jews
> fall at your feet and acknowledge that I love you.
> Because you have endured patiently, I will keep
> you from the trial that is going to come upon the
> Earth. I Am coming soon. Remain faithful so that
> no one can take your Crown. If you have an ear,
> hear what the Holy Spirit says to the Churches,
> and I will write My name on him.

Jesus held the key of David. The meaning is obscure, but it is similar to wording in Isaiah 22:20–25. Eliakim was King Hezekiah's finance minister. But we know that the One who holds these powers is Jesus. Jesus is the root and the offspring of David, and He was holding the door to heaven open for the Philadelphians. Philadelphia is the second church with whom Jesus found no fault. He loved them, and they would receive a crown. Like the church of Smyrna, they would receive the crown of life.

Like the church of Smyrna, apparently the "synagogue of Satan" was harassing them, but those villains would bow at the feet of the people of the church at Philadelphia. The Christians at Philadelphia were faithful, but they were persecuted. Eleven Christians were martyred there in AD 156.

Today the town of Alaşehir sits on the ruins of Philadelphia at the foot of a mountain. The population of Alaşehir is less than fifty thousand, but they have a geothermal power plant. Important products are tobacco, raisins, and fruit. Water from their mineral springs is also an important product. It is a Muslim city with around forty-five mosques. A titular bishop of the Catholic Church remains. A titular bishop is not over a diocese but oversees a community of the faithful.

> REVELATION 3:14–22. To the Angel of the
> Church of Laodicea: I Am the Amen. I Am the
> faithful and true ruler of God's creation. I know
> that you are neither hot nor cold. You are luke-
> warm and I am about to spit you out. You think

you are rich and do not need anything, but you are wretched, poor, blind, and naked. Buy refined gold from Me so you can be rich. Buy white clothes from Me so you can cover your shame. Buy eye medicine from Me so that you can see. I rebuke those I love, so be earnest and repent. I stand at the door and knock. If you can hear My voice and open the door, I will come in and eat with you. If you have an ear, hear what the Holy Spirit says to the Churches. If you overcome, I will give you the right to sit on My throne with Me.

Do not resent it when God corrects you, because His punishment is proof of His love. As your Father, He disciplines you to make you better. (Proverbs 3:11–12)

The city of Laodicea was a wealthy commercial and banking city, and it was known for the production of an eye and ear medicine. It was destroyed in AD 600 by an earthquake.

The city was on the eastern slope of the Honaz Mountain, which is the highest peak in the area. The Honaz Fault is a graben fault (or crack in Earth's crust) that continues to produce a lot of earthquakes or tremors. One wall of the fault moves upward, and the other wall of the fault moves downward.

Jesus loved the people of the church of Laodicea, but they were not in love with Him. They believed, but they were self-satisfied. They were not going anywhere. They were too comfortable, so they were not passionate. We like hot coffee or iced tea, but we do not like a mouthful of lukewarm water.

Today the city that sits there is named Denizli, with a population of half a million people, but it hosts two million tourists who flock to its thermal spas every year. It is a bustling, modern, industrial city. It is Muslim, but there are a few converts to Christianity.

CHAPTER 4

Revelation 4:1–11

There are many mansions where My Father lives. I Am going to prepare for your coming. When everything is ready, I will come and get you, so you can be with Me.

—John 14:2–3

REVELATION 4:1–5. I see a door standing open in Heaven. The voice I first heard speaking to me like a trumpet said, "Come in and see what is about to occur." Immediately, the Holy Spirit engulfs me and transports me to Heaven. I see God sitting on His Throne. God's appearance is like the gemstones jasper and sardonyx, and He is surrounded by an emerald rainbow. There are seven lampstands burning before the Throne of God, and I see 24 Elders wearing gold crowns and clothed in white robes sitting on 24 thrones surrounding the Throne of God.

Here, we are given a glimpse of the Rapture (1 Thessalonians 4:17). The Rapture is an impending event that Paul described to us.

The Lord will come out from Heaven and with the trumpet call of God. The dead in Christ will rise first, and then we who are still alive will be caught up with them in the clouds to meet Him in the air. We will be with the Lord forever. (1 Thessalonians 4:16–17)

God has given us guidance so that we can look forward to what is coming. On Mount Sinai, God instructed Moses to establish feasts to commemorate certain events (Leviticus 23). The Israelites did not know it, but these feasts did not just mark events in their own lives. These feasts were also prophesies of future events. Most of those prophesies have already been fulfilled. The Lord had a plan.

Feasts of the Lord

Passover, or Pesach (Leviticus 23:5), began when God forced Pharaoh to allow Moses to lead the children of Israel out of Egypt. The Israelite families sacrificed a lamb for that first Passover. They were instructed to paint its blood on their doors. That night the angel of death passed over the homes which had the lamb's blood over the doors, but killed the firstborn of all the Egyptian homes, causing Pharaoh to allow the Israelites to leave. Passover was fulfilled when Jesus Christ, the Lamb of God, was crucified (John 19:17–37). We paint His blood on our doorposts, which protects us from the second death (Revelation 20:6).

Unleavened Bread or Haghamatzot (Leviticus 23:6–8) began when the children of Israel departed from Egypt. They did not have time to allow their bread to rise. They just cooked it, ate it quickly, and moved on. Unleavened Bread was fulfilled when Jesus Christ lay dead in the grave, but His body did not decay (John 19:38–42).

Firstfruits or Yom Habikkurim (Leviticus 23:9–14) immediately followed Unleavened Bread and celebrated the first grain reaped in the barley harvest. Firstfruits was fulfilled with the resurrection of Jesus Christ (John 20). He was the first to be resurrected from the grave in His glorified body, fulfilling the prophecy of the Feast of Firstfruits. Christians will be raptured with their glorified bodies.

Pentecost or Shavout (Leviticus 23:15–22) falls fifty days after Firstfruits, and it marked the first grain reaped in the wheat harvest.

Pentecost was fulfilled when the Holy Spirit came upon the disciples of Jesus Christ and entered believers when the disciples shared God's Word with them (Acts 2:1–4). Prior to Pentecost, the Holy Spirit would come to individuals from time to time, but He did not live within them. This is how it will probably be on Earth following the Rapture. Since Pentecost, Christians have the support of the Holy Spirit of God living within them (1 Corinthians 3:16).

Three of these holy days remain to be fulfilled.

Trumpets or Rosh Hashanah (Leviticus 23:23–25) marked the beginning of the New Year. The shofar, or ram's horn, was blown one hundred times to remind the Israelites that they were entering ten days of repentance. Trumpets will be fulfilled when the Lord Jesus Christ appears in the clouds and calls Christians with the voice of a trumpet to come live with Him in the place He is preparing for His bride (1 Thessalonians 4:16–17).

Day of Atonement or Yom Kippur (Leviticus 23:26–32) is the only one of these Holy Days which is not a feast. The Israelites were commanded to cleanse themselves, and to deny themselves. Atonement will be fulfilled at the end of Daniel's seventieth week (Daniel 9:24–27), when Jesus Christ returns to establish His millennial kingdom. The Israelites will look upon Him and mourn as for an only child (Zechariah 12:10).

Tabernacles or Sukkot (Leviticus 23:33–36) was celebrated as a sacred assembly. The Israelites traveled to Jerusalem for the feast. They built shelters and camped out in the streets of Jerusalem and on the surrounding hillsides. Tabernacles will be fulfilled when Jesus Christ returns and tabernacles with His people for one thousand years (Revelation 20:1–4).

Jesus promised (Revelation 3:10) that He would protect His Christians from the hour of trial, which will engulf the whole world during the seventieth week of Daniel's vision. He will take us, His bride, to heaven to be with Him forever. That is what the Rapture is all about.

We see the wedding taking place just before Christ departs heaven to fulfill Sukkot—the Feast of Tabernacles, the second coming.

> Let us rejoice and give Him Glory! The time for
> the wedding of the Lamb has come and His Bride
> has made herself ready. She is wearing fine linen,
> bright and clean. Fine linen stands for the good
> deeds of the saints. (Revelation 19:7–8)

Who are the twenty-four elders with thrones surrounding the throne of God? Elders were capable, godly, honest men who could resolve disputes among the people (Exodus 18:13–27).

Some people believe that these elders in heaven can only be Christians. They are wearing white robes and have gold crowns on their heads. Each had a harp and a golden vial containing the incense of the prayers of God's people, and they sing a new song (Revelation 5:8–10). Please note that these elders were already there when the Rapture occurred and John suddenly found himself in heaven. Remember, ever since Jesus Christ completed God's plan for our salvation, the spirits of Christians have been going to heaven (Luke 23:39–43). Also, it seems that God has been transporting Israelites to be with Him in heaven all along. The elders will be very special people who have faithfully served God the Father and God the Son with the help of God the Holy Spirit.

Some people believe that twelve of the elders are patriarchs, and twelve of the elders are apostles. That is feasible, because the names on the gates of heaven are the names of the twelve tribes of Israel. The names of the twelve apostles are written on the foundation of heaven (Revelation 21:10–14).

Heaven. There is no promise of "you will always be with Me" in the Old Testament. Heaven was God's home. Before Jesus Christ completed our salvation two thousand years ago, it seems that the righteous went into a comforting holding place which Jesus called Abraham's bosom, while the unrighteous entered a hot place, which Jesus called Hades. Luke recorded our Lord's teaching about life after death.

> There was a rich man who lived each day in
> luxury. A beggar named Lazarus lay at his door
> begging for scraps from the rich man's table...

> The beggar died and angels carried him to be
> with Abraham in the place of the righteous dead.
> When the rich man died, his soul went into
> Hades. In his torment, he could see Lazarus far
> away in Abraham's Bosom across a great chasm.
> (Luke 16:19–23)

The Hebrew name of the holding place for the souls of the dead
was *Sheol*. The Greek word for it was *Hades*. Jesus described Sheol as
two separate places: "Abraham's Bosom" was a resting place for the
righteous, and a hot place of torment housed the unrighteous dead.

But it seems that not everyone went to Sheol. We know of a few
exceptions. We know of two people who lived so close to God that
they did not taste death: Enoch and Elijah.

> Enoch was 65 years old when his son Methuselah
> was born. Then he lived another 300 years in fel-
> lowship with God, and he produced other sons
> and daughters. When he had lived 365 years
> walking with God, he was not. God took him.
> (Genesis 5:21–24)

> As they walked along talking, suddenly a char-
> iot of fire drawn by horses of fire appeared. They
> were separated when it drove between them, and
> Elijah was carried by a whirlwind into heaven.
> Elisha saw it and cried out, "My father! The
> chariot of Israel and the charioteers!" (2 Kings
> 2:11–12)

The Lord probably did not send a chariot down to give these
two very special people a ride to Abraham's Bosom. Surely the Lord
brought Enoch and Elijah to live with Him in heaven. Maybe these
two very special people will again serve the Lord as prophets during
the final seven years of Daniel's prophecy (Daniel 9:26–27).

> I will give My two witnesses power to prophesy
> 1,260 days clothed in sackcloth... When they
> complete the 3 1/2 years of their testimony,
> the tyrant who comes out of the bottomless
> pit will declare war against them and kill them.
> (Revelation 11:3–7)

Will the antichrist be able to kill these two prophets, because they have not previously suffered death? God has always had a plan.

When Elisha said, "The chariot of Israel," was he referring to the patriarch Jacob, who God had named Israel (Genesis 32:28)? Did God send Jacob down to give Elijah a ride to heaven? Is Jacob also living with God in heaven?

We know of another person who probably has been living in heaven with the Lord through the ages. Some of the apostles saw Moses and Elijah meeting with Jesus on Mount Tabor, known by us as the Mount of Transfiguration. Has Moses also been with God in heaven through the millennia?

> Six days later, Jesus took Peter, James, and John to
> the top of a high mountain. As they watched, His
> appearance changed. His face shone like the sun
> and his clothes became bright white. Suddenly
> Moses and Elijah appeared and were talking with
> Him. (Matthew 17:1–3)

Are Enoch and Elijah and Moses among the elders sitting on thrones in the presence of God wearing gold crowns? There are probably many more Old Testament heroes who have been at home in heaven with God down through the ages.

During Daniel's seventieth week (Daniel 9:26–27), while the antichrist is in charge on Earth, Christians will be in heaven celebrating the fulfillment of their betrothal to Jesus.

> Then I heard the shouting of a huge crowd, like
> great thunder, "Praise the Lord, our Almighty

God who reigns. Rejoice and be glad and honor
Him, for the time has come for the wedding ban-
quet of the Lamb and His bride, who is prepared.
She wears the cleanest white and the finest linen.
The fine linen is the good deeds done by God's
people. (Revelation 19:6–8)

At this moment, God is sitting on His throne in heaven. His
appearance is awesome. God's very appearance is like the gemstones
jasper, and sardonyx. These are translucent multicolored stones that
glow in His holy light. God is surrounded by an emerald rainbow.
The emerald is a beautiful green crystal that refracts the holy light
and projects rainbows all around.

Not only are the streets of heaven pure gold, but we will be
surrounded by the beauty of all the other enduring treasures. God
created these treasures, and He is surrounded by them. The home
which Jesus is preparing for us will be made of these treasures. The
very foundations of the New Jerusalem will be gemstones. The walls
of the city will be gemstones.

One of the seven angels who had poured out his
flask of the wrath of God comes to me. "I will
show you the Bride." He takes me to a mountain
peak and I watch the New Jerusalem, home of
the Bride, as it descends from the skies. It appears
to be a clear crystal cube filled with the Glory of
God. The angel measures the City with a gold
rod. The sides of the cube measure 1500 miles
in length, in width, and in height. The walls
made of diamond are 216 feet thick, with 12
gates, each made of a single pearl. There are three
gates on each of the eastern, northern, southern,
and western sides of the City. The names of the
12 Tribes of Israel are written on the gates. The
names of the 12 Apostles are written on the 12
foundation stones made of jasper, sapphire, chal-

cedony, emerald, sardonyx, carnelian, chrysolite, beryl, topaz, chrysoprase, turquoise, and amethyst. The City Is made of pure gold, as transparent as glass. (Revelation 21:9–21)

REVELATION 4:6–11. I see flashes of lightning and rumbles of thunder coming from the Throne of God. Seven blazing lampstands which are the seven Spirits of God stand before the Throne which sits beside a crystal sea. There are four living creatures with many eyes moving around the Throne. The first creature looks like a lion, and the second looks like a calf. The third creature looks like a man, and the fourth is flying above like an eagle. All of these creatures have six wings. Day and night these creatures glorify God, chanting, "Holy, Holy, Holy Lord God Almighty, Who was, and is, and is to come." The 24 elders respond by kneeling and worshiping God, praying, "O Lord, You are Worthy to receive glory, honor, and power. You created all things, and all things exist by Your Will."

The winged creatures encircling the throne of God are cherubim. When God expelled Adam and Eve from the garden of Eden, He placed cherubim at the east to guard against their returning to eat from the tree of life (Genesis 3:23–24).

When Moses was on Mount Sinai receiving the Law from God, he also received instructions for the construction of the ark of the covenant. God told Moses to make two cherubim from hammered gold and to place them facing each other over the cover of the ark. God would meet Moses between those cherubim (Exodus 25:17–22).

Ezekiel saw God's chariot accompanied by cherubim on two different occasions (Ezekiel 1 and 10). He described them as having the faces of an ox, a man, a lion, and an eagle, similar to John's description here. Ezekiel described God's throne as beautiful sapphire blue, and he described God as having the appearance of a man, glowing bronze and fire, encircled by a rainbow (Ezekiel 1:26–28).

Around 740 BC, the prophet Isaiah also saw the throne of God encircled by creatures, which he called seraphim. John's description of cherubim in Revelation is very similar to Isaiah's account of seraphim in that they have six wings.

> The year King Uzziah died, I saw the Lord. He was seated on a Throne and the train of His robe filled the Temple. Mighty Seraphim, each having six wings, hovered about Him. They sang, "Holy, Holy, Holy is the Lord Almighty! The whole earth is filled with His glory!" Their singing shook the Temple and it was filled with smoke. (Isaiah 6:1–4)

CHAPTER 5

Revelation 5:1–14

O Lord, Your right hand is majestic in power. O Lord,
Your right hand has shattered the enemy.

—Exodus 16:6

REVELATION 5:1–5. God is holding a scroll
in His right hand. There is writing on both sides
of the scroll, and it is sealed with seven seals. A
mighty Angel asks in a loud voice, "Who is worthy to break the seals and open the scroll?" I weep
because no one on Earth is worthy, but one of the
Elders tells me, "Do not weep! The Lion of the
Tribe of Judah, the Root of David is able to open
the scroll."

God is sitting on His throne, and He is holding a scroll in His
right hand. The scroll is held closed with seven wax seals. The
scroll contains God's plan for the judgment that will be executed
upon those who set themselves against Him. Our omnificent God
created us in His image (Genesis 1:26–27). He did not create us to
be perfect. When God created us, He gave us the ability to choose
Him, or to choose not to follow Him—we can choose to sin. We can
choose to honor and obey God. Without the ability to choose, we
would only be robots. Since God is omniscient, He knows the past

and the future. He does not control our decisions, but He can see the choices we will make.

> O transgressors, don't forget the many times when I clearly told you what would happen. I Am God. There is no other like Me. I have declared the end from ancient times. All that I say will happen, because My will shall come to pass. (Isaiah 46:8–10)

There are seven seals on the scroll. Seven is a blessed number, associated with completion.

> The Heavens and the Earth and all the creation were finished. God rested from His work on the seventh day. God blessed the seventh day and made it holy. (Genesis 2:1–3)

God's scribe had written a section of the scroll and then sealed that section of the scroll with a wax seal. Then the scribe wrote the next section and sealed that section of the scroll. There are seven writings on the scroll to be unsealed, one at a time. Since this is God's plan, it can only be revealed by someone able to execute God's judgment. There are great people and beings in Heaven, but who can measure up to the task of executing God's judgment?

John was an apostle. He knew Jesus Christ when He walked on the Earth. He knew that Jesus Christ died as our Passover Lamb, sacrificing Himself for our sins. Before he was transported to heaven, John saw Jesus Christ standing among the seven lampstands, but he has not seen Jesus Christ in the throne room of God up in heaven. He is distraught, because he knows no one other than God Himself in this panorama before him is worthy to reveal His everlasting judgment. But God is holding it out, asking for someone worthy to open it. John knows that certainly he is not worthy, even though he was redeemed by the sacrifice of Jesus, and even though he was martyred for teaching about God's Son, Jesus. Tears form in John's eyes.

We all have sinned. We all fall short of God's
glory. (Romans 3:23)

One of the elders wearing a gold crown leaves his throne and
comes to comfort John. He reminds John that the Lord Jesus Christ
is worthy to disclose God's words to us. In fact, Jesus *is* the Word
of God. In the first verses of Genesis, we are shown three distinct
aspects of God.

In the beginning, God our FATHER created
the Heavens and the Earth. The Earth was void
and without form. The Holy SPIRIT of God
hovered over the waters. Then God SAID [The
Word of God, The Lamb of God, The Light of
the World], "Let there be Light," and there was
Light. (Genesis 1:1–3)

We are enlightened by the Word of God. John had spent time
thinking about that. In fact, the Gospel of John opens with some
clarification on the creation.

In the beginning was the Word. The Word was
with God, and the Word was God. Through
Him all things were made. Without Him, nothing was made. In Him was Life, and that Life was
the Light of men. (John 1:1–4)

Jesus is the Word of God. In His revelation, He is pictured as
having the sword of the Word of God in His mouth.

He holds seven stars in His right hand, and
a sharp double-edged sword comes from His
mouth. (Revelation 1:16)

The elder calls Jesus the "Lion of the Tribe of Judah" and the
"Root of David." The twelve sons of Jacob (Israel) were the patri-

archs of the twelve tribes of Israel. Reuben was Jacob's oldest son, but because of his rebellion, he was not chosen to lead the messianic line (Genesis 49:1–4). Jacob's fourth son, Judah, became the messianic line, as prophesied by Jacob himself. Jesus the Messiah is the "Lion of the Tribe of Judah."

> Your brothers shall praise you, Judah. You shall destroy your enemies, and your brothers shall bow down before you. You have consumed your prey and have settled down as a lion. Who can challenge you? The scepter shall not depart from Judah until Shiloh [the Messiah] comes. (Genesis 49:8–10)

Jesus also is the "Root of David." Jesse was David's father. Mary, the mother of Jesus, was a descendant of Jesse and of David. But Jesus was at the creation of the universe long before King David existed. Back to Adam, through Seth and Enoch, Noah and Shem, Abraham and Isaac, Jesse and David, the Word of God was with them all.

> A Rod will come up from the root of Jesse. A Branch will come up from his stump, and the Spirit of the Lord will rest on Him: The Spirit of wisdom, understanding, counsel, might, knowledge, righteousness, and the fear of the Lord… With righteousness He will judge the poor. (Isaiah 11:1–4)

Here, Isaiah also enumerates the sevenfold Spirit of God: Wisdom, Understanding, Counsel, Might, Knowledge, Fear (Awe) of the Lord, and Righteousness.

The Gospel of Matthew at 1:1–17 gives us the line of Joseph, husband of Mary and stepfather of Jesus; that is the kingly line through Solomon. The Gospel of Luke at 3:23–38, gives us the true messianic line of Jesus through David's son Nathan and down to Heli, father of Jesus's mother, Mary.

REVELATION 5:6–14. I see the Lamb who had been slain standing before the Throne of God. He has seven horns and seven eyes. The horns and eyes are the seven-fold Spirit of God. He reaches out and takes the scroll from the right hand of God, and the Elders and the Cherubim kneel down before Him singing, "You are worthy to open the scroll, because You died and Your blood has purchased people from every Nation who are a kingdom of priests for God." Millions of Angels and everyone in Heaven and on Earth are singing, "The blessing and honor and glory belong to God and to the Lamb forever!"

The Lamb is standing before the throne of God. Even though John did not see Him at first, Jesus Christ has been there all along. Upon His resurrection, He first showed Himself to Mary Magdalene. He gave specific instructions to comfort His followers. (John 20:1–8). Jesus was on His way to show Himself to God—He was on His way to this throne room of God (John 20:17). After showing Himself to God, Jesus spent forty days with His followers on Earth, and then ascended back to heaven (Acts 1:3–13). He has spent the last two thousand years in Heaven, and will remain there until He returns to Earth to begin His millennial reign (Revelation 19:11–21). Yes, the Lamb has scars.

He was wounded for our transgressions, and bruised for our sins. He bore the punishment which bought our peace. By His wounds we are healed. (Isaiah 53:5)

John perceives that the Lamb has seven horns. A horn denotes power or government. Seven horns denotes complete power. Jesus Christ is omnipotent; He has complete power.

John perceives that the Lamb has seven eyes. Jesus Christ is omniscient; Jesus Christ sees everything. He has complete knowledge of everything hidden.

Remember, Isaiah has already told us that the sevenfold Spirit of God is the Spirit of Wisdom, Understanding, Counsel, Might, Knowledge, and the Fear of the Lord (Isaiah 11:1–4). He is all all-powerful and all-knowing.

> Woe to those who try to hide their plans from God and conceal what they do in darkness. They think He does not see what they do. (Isaiah 29:15)

These wounds suffered by the Lamb of God were part of God's plan from the beginning. When Adam and Eve disobeyed God and ate from the tree of knowledge of good and evil in the garden of Eden (Genesis 3:1–7), their eyes were opened up to their sins, so they hid from God. Animals were sacrificed to hide their nakedness (Genesis 3:21). God established animal sacrifice to hide the sins of men. These animal sacrifices pointed toward the sacrifice to be made by Jesus. Jesus Christ willingly and knowingly endured these wounds because He loved us (John 3:16—the center of the Bible). Jesus Christ is worthy to execute the judgments of God.

His wounds were fatal. They were administered by men (John 19:1–42), but the men could not have laid a hand on God the Son if He had not been the willing sacrifice for our sins. He had always completely been a part of God's plan for our redemption. He was our willing sacrifice. Jesus came as the sacrificial Lamb the first time. He will come as the Lion when He returns. He came the first time to redeem us. The definition of redeem is to buy back something ransomed.

> They trust in their riches and boast of their wealth, but they cannot redeem their brother by paying a ransom for him. The redemption of the soul is precious, and no payment is ever enough for everlasting life. (Psalm, 49:6–9)

Only the ransom paid by Jesus Christ is sufficient.

Though He was God, He made Himself nothing, taking the form of a human servant. He humbled Himself and was obedient to death on a cross. Therefore, God has exalted Him to the highest place and given Him a name above every name. At the name of Jesus every knee will bow in Heaven and on Earth, and under the Earth. Every tongue shall confess that Jesus Christ is Lord, to the Glory of God the Father. (Philippians 2:6–11)

In a vision to Zechariah, God revealed that He would send His branch and would remove the iniquity from the land. God would place a Precious Stone with seven eyes before Joshua, the high priest, and that Precious Stone would bring peace to the land in one day.

O Joshua, you are symbolic of things to come. I have set a Precious Stone with seven eyes before you, and I will engrave an inscription on it. I will remove sin from the Land in one day. In that day you will invite your neighbor to sit beneath your vine and share your fig tree. (Zechariah 3:8–10)

Jesus Christ accepts the scroll from God. He is worthy to dispense God's judgment, and He agrees to accept the assignment. The Lamb of God will execute God's judgment against those who have rebelled against God. The elders kneel before the Lamb, because He alone is worthy to execute God's judgment. They acknowledge that He is worthy because of His willing sacrifice on our behalf. These wise men who once walked on the Earth and had firsthand knowledge of the sins of man, and of their own sins acknowledge that the blood of Jesus Christ has redeemed us.

Suddenly, everyone in heaven is singing, "Honor and Glory belong to God and to the Lamb forever." There are millions of voices raised in praise of our God. Daniel was privileged with a vision of this moment in heaven as judgment is about to be dispensed.

As I watched, thrones were set in place and the Ancient of Days was seated. His clothing and hair were white as snow. His throne was flaming. A river of fire flowed before Him, and 10,000 times 10,000 stood before Him. The books were opened. (Daniel 7:9–10)

CHAPTER 6

Revelation 6:1–17

On the twenty-fourth day of the eleventh month in the second
year of the reign of Darius, the Lord showed me a vision. A man
riding a red horse was among the myrtle trees in a ravine, and
a red, a brown, and a white horse were behind him. I asked,
"Who are they?" The man explained, 'The Lord has sent them
throughout the Earth, and they have found the world at peace."

—Zechariah 1:7–11

REVELATION 6:1–2. The Lamb breaks the first
seal on the scroll, and one of the four Seraphim
calls out with a voice that sounds like thunder,
"Come!" A White Horse whose rider carries a
bow appears. The horseman is crowned world
leader, and he gallops away to conquer.

T he rider on the white horse unleashed by the opening of the first
seal is not a hero. He is not one of the Lord's horsemen. He is
the false prince of peace. He is the antichrist. Early on, he will make
a treaty with Israel. This may be when the temple is rebuilt. We know
there will be a temple, and that it will be Israel's place of worship in
the first half of the Tribulation.

He will make a covenant with many for seven
years. In the middle of the seven years he will

43

> end sacrifices and offerings. On a wing of the
> Temple he will set up an abomination that will
> cause the Temple to be desolate until his decreed
> end. (Daniel 9:27)

The seventieth week of Daniel's prophecy has begun, known as the Tribulation because of the great hardships that will fall on those remaining on Earth. The Rapture (Nissuin) has occurred—the Bridegroom has carried His bride home. For the next seven years Christians are in seclusion in heaven with the Bridegroom for the consummation of their marriage. The final seven years preceding the second coming of Jesus Christ has begun. (See chapter 19.) The judgments have commenced, and focus has shifted from heaven to the Earth. The antichrist is the world's leader with the aid of Satan (Revelation 13:1–4). The abomination that causes desolation is probably a statue of the antichrist set up by the false prophet, who demands that the people worship the statue (Revelation 13:11–12).

The Tribulation, Daniel's seventieth week, will last for seven years. The remaining seven years preceding the second coming of Jesus Christ will be a time of constant war. The Israelites, including those who have accepted Jesus Christ, will remain on Earth. The Holy Spirit has departed the Earth, and the messianic Israelites will witness to God's wife during the Tribulation. The rider of the white horse is not a hero—he is the antichrist, and he will fight desperately in a last-ditch effort to defeat God's plan and God's people.

> REVELATION 6:3–4. As we watch, the Lamb
> unrolls the scroll and breaks the second seal, and
> the second Seraphim calls out, "Come!" A rider
> on a Red Horse appears and he is given a long
> sword with which he takes peace from the whole
> earth. He will make men kill each other.

A fiery red horse gallops onto the scene, ready to do battle. The rider is given a weapon of war-a long sword. Will the rider of the red horse fight with the rider of the white horse or against him? What may begin as an attack against Israel will spread to worldwide battles. The next seven years will be lawless chaos. The sword indicates that there will be constant war for the entire Tribulation. The rampant killing of those remaining on the Earth has begun. The stench of the pale horse, death, is everywhere.

War does not just kill people. The weapons of war also destroy the land and pollute the air and the water. Food crops are ravaged. Trees are downed and cease to produce oxygen. Deadly carbon monoxide and carbon dioxide dilute the oxygen that people breathe.

> REVELATION 6:5–6. The Lamb breaks the third seal on the scroll, and the third Seraphim calls, "Come!" A Black Horse whose rider is carrying a scale in his hand appears. The third Seraphim pronounces, "You can purchase a loaf of bread or three pounds of flour for a day's wages. Protect the wine or oil."

Destruction of food crops means hunger. There are fewer and fewer people on the Earth because Christians are in heaven, and the people remaining on Earth are dying by the thousands in the constant fighting. There are fewer and fewer farmers. Insects, which are required to pollinate their crops, are becoming extinct. The good farm land is destroyed by the weapons of war, and the environment is so hostile that crops cannot survive. War destroys trade and commerce. Transportation is disrupted. Distribution resources cease to exist. Whatever food remains cannot be accessed by the people. Prices for food are so inflated that people cannot purchase whatever may come to market. Hunger is widespread, and the weakened, hungry people fall ill.

> REVELATION 6:7–8. As the Black horse gallops away, The Lamb breaks the fourth seal and we hear the fourth Seraphim call, "Come!" A rider named Death approaches, riding a Pale Horse. Close behind him is another horse whose

rider is named Hades. Death and Hades are given power to kill one-fourth of the Earth. They will use war, hunger, disease, and wild animals to kill the inhabitants of the Earth.

Global warming has become acute, exacerbated by the exhausts of war machines, by the constant explosions and fires and burning buildings, and by the accumulation of carbon monoxide. People are pale and weak from pollution and hunger. Shelter is at a premium cost. Inflation is rampant. If anyone has money, there is nothing to buy. They try to flee the rubble and the famine. They become refugees with nowhere to go. They eat anything they can find. They fight hungry animals for rotting carrion. They become cannibalistic. People are dying in the streets.

REVELATION 6:9–11. The Lamb opens the fifth seal and our attention is focused on the Altar. Beneath the Altar are the souls of the martyrs who have been killed for preaching the Gospel. We hear their anguish as they pray, "O Holy, Sovereign Lord, when will You judge the enemies who have killed us? When will You avenge our blood?" The martyrs are covered with white robes and are encouraged to wait a little longer until the remainder of those who will be killed can join them.

Although Christians departed the Earth at the Rapture, the messianic Israelites have remained on Earth to witness to God's wife (Revelation 7:1–8). The Lord has also placed His two witnesses on Earth to declare His salvation through the first half of Daniel's seventieth week (Revelation 12:1–12). There are millions of people who grew up in church but did not embrace Christ. There is nothing like facing death to draw someone's attention to God. Many people have turned to the Lord during the Tribulation. Since Satan is in control, those who turn to God will be persecuted and killed. More martyrs will come out of the Tribulation to join those martyrs who are already under the altar in heaven.

> REVELATION 6:12–17. A great earthquake shakes the Earth as the Lamb breaks the sixth seal. The sun is darkened, and the moon becomes blood red. The skies disappear and stars are falling. The mountains shake and the islands are shifted. We see everyone, from the military leaders and the world's rulers to the poorest of the people all hiding in caves. They are terrified and they beg the mountains to fall on them and crush them. They are hiding from God and the anger of the Lamb. "Who can survive the wrath of the Lord?"

John is up in heaven looking down at the developing disaster on Earth. In heaven, he sees Jesus break the sixth seal, and the whole Earth shakes. John calls it an earthquake, but many Bible scholars believe it is probably nuclear war. In the AD first century, John had no words to describe nuclear war, so that speculation may be correct. When the Lamb released the red horse, peace was banished from the Earth. Nuclear weapons are being deployed. We are dealing with the wrath of God here. He can bring an asteroid against the Earth. Or He can unleash a great tectonic event that would rearrange the entire New Roman Empire. Regardless of God's methods, His intent is realized, because man's worst instincts are no longer restrained.

A great cloud of ash is released into the atmosphere which darkens the sun. Darkness covers the Earth. The moon is visible, but its reflected light glows red through the quantity of ash unleashed into the atmosphere. The inhabitants of the Earth see falling stars. The "stars" are probably a meteor storm, but they could be bombs falling.

It is expected that the Rapture of the bride of Christ will fulfill the prophecy of Rosh Hashanah, or the Feast of Trumpets (Leviticus 22:23–25), which occurs in either September or October every year. Since stars cannot literally fall to the Earth, the falling stars probably are meteors. Meteors occur when the Earth travels through debris left behind in outer space by asteroids and comets. When that debris encounters Earth's atmosphere, it burns and its remains fall to the Earth. In November of each year, the Earth experiences a Leonid meteor shower, during which approximately fifteen meteorites per hour strike the Earth. Every thirty-three years, the number of meteors encountered increases to approximately fifteen meteorites per second. Those events are called a Leonid meteor storm. The last Leonid meteor storm occurred in 2010.

The great earthquake has literally destroyed every building. People cannot hide from earthquakes in buildings. Those who do are buried alive in the debris. Those who escape (both the important people and the ordinary people) will flee and will try to hide underground. The people know that this is God's anger, but they do not turn to Him. People are not praying to God; the people are hiding from God in the mountains. But you cannot hide from the wrath of God.

> That terrible day is near. It comes swiftly. Strong men will weep bitterly. The Wrath of God is poured out, and it is a day of terrible distress and anguish. It is a day of ruin and desolation, of darkness and gloom, a day of trumpet calls and battle cries. Your fortifications fall. I will make you as helpless as a blind man because you have sinned against the Lord. Your blood will be poured out and your bodies will rot in the dust. (Zephaniah 1:14–17)

Jesus Himself told us that this great event is just a precursor of the final great shaking of the Earth, which will occur as He mounts His own white horse to return to rule on Earth for one thousand years. At that time, "A mighty angel will pick up a boulder and throw it into the ocean" (Revelation 18:21). In his vision, John saw this final asteroid striking the Earth. Jesus told us,

> At the end of the Tribulation the sun will be darkened, and the moon will not give light. The

heavens will be shaken and the stars will seem to fall. And then at last the signal of My coming will appear in the heavens and there will be deep mourning all around the Earth. (Matthew 24:29–30)

CHAPTER 7

Revelation 7:1–17

He made the world, yet the world did not recognize Him. He
came to His own, yet own did not receive Him. But all who did
believe in Him received the right to become children of God.

—John 1:10–12

REVELATION 7:1–8. Angels are standing to the
north, the south, the east, and the west holding
back the winds. Another angel holding the Seal of
God approaches and instructs them to do nothing until God's seal can be imprinted on the foreheads of His servants. The number who will be
given God's seal is 144,000. They are Children of
Israel and I watch as 144,000 Israelites—12,000
from each of the 12 Tribes of Israel—receive the
Seal of God on their foreheads.

Suddenly, everything pauses. The winds cease to blow. Not a leaf
rustles in the trees. The ocean is as smooth as glass. The Earth
is holding its breath. Just before the turmoil on Earth begins, the
universe stands at attention while the children of Israel, who witness
for the Lord during the Tribulation, receive the seal of God. These
are messianic Israelites who were not Raptured with the church,
although they believe in Jesus Christ. They will remain on Earth
through much of the Tribulation. They are very special people who

are commissioned by God to witness to His wife (Hosea 2:16–17). The children of Israel must endure the Tribulation because they did not recognize God's Son, who came to them two thousand years ago. Satan will come against them with all his strength. They will be attacked and abused and martyred, but they will serve God. They will fulfill their commission.

The twelve tribes listed in Revelation 7 do not exactly match up with the twelve sons of Jacob (Israel) as listed in Genesis 29–30. God will seal twelve thousand witnesses from each of the tribes of Reuben, Simeon, Levi, Judah, Manasseh, Naphtali, Gad, Asher, Issachar, Zebulun, Joseph, and Benjamin. In this list in Revelation, Dan is replaced by Manasseh, son of Joseph. There is discrepancy between this list and the list of the tribes blessed by Moses (Deuteronomy 33). There is discrepancy between this list and in the list of the tribes given their portion of the promised land by Joshua (Joshua 13–17). There is discrepancy between this list and the list of tribes given land during the millennial reign of Jesus Christ as set out in Ezekiel's prophecy (Ezekiel 48). The Tribulation list of the twelve tribes of Israel is probably the list for all eternity.

REVELATION 7:9–17. Then a multitude of souls from every Nation gathers around The Throne of God, all wearing white robes and waving palm fronds. They kneel before the Throne of God, worshiping Him saying, "Praise, and glory, and wisdom, and thanksgiving, and honor, and power be given to God forever. Amen!" An Elder asks me, "Do you know who these souls are? They are all martyrs coming out of the Great Tribulation which is occurring on Earth. Their robes are washed in the Blood of the Lamb. They will serve Him and God will shelter them. They will never be hungry or thirsty again, because the Lamb will be their Shepherd. He will feed them and lead them to the Water of Life, and God will wipe away their tears."

These martyrs are in heaven, dressed in white and waving palm fronds. At the beginning of the Messiah's final week on Earth, Jesus Christ fulfilled a prophecy, which was made by Zechariah some five hundred years earlier.

> O My people, shout with joy! Your King is com-
> ing! He is the righteous Victor! Yet he is lowly,
> riding on a donkey's colt. (Zechariah 9:9)

Kings did not ride on horses. Horses were the beasts of battle. Kings rode on donkeys. Some one thousand years earlier, when David was on his deathbed, he arranged for his son Solomon to be crowned as the next king of Israel. David instructed that Solomon was to ride in state on King David's personal mule for the coronation (1 Kings 1:32–35). Just before His sacrifice, when Jesus rode in state on a donkey, it was not humility. This was Jesus Christ proclaiming His kingship!

> Jesus found a young donkey and sat upon it, as it
> was written. (John 12:14)

Jesus fulfilled Zechariah's prophecy riding as the Eternal King of all people, and they were also waving palm fronds. Some two thousand years ago, when the crowds heard that Jesus was about to enter Jerusalem for the week of Passover, they cut palm fronds and met Him, shouting, "Hosanna! Blessed is He who comes in the name of the Lord. Blessed is the King of Israel!" (John 12:12–13). That day is still commemorated as Palm Sunday.

As soon as God seals His 144,000 witnesses, martyrs begin to appear before the throne of God. The antichrist has wasted no time, and he is attacking God's people with full force.

> The Lord declares, "Two-thirds will be struck
> down, but one-third will remain in the Land of
> Israel. I will bring those who remain through the
> fire and refine them like silver and gold. They

will call on My Name and I will answer them. I
will say, "They are My people," and they will say,
"The Lord is our God." (Zechariah 13:8–9)

An elder askes John if he understands the makeup of this crowd
standing before the throne of God waving palm fronds. He explains
that they are all martyrs coming to heaven from the Great Tribulation,
which is taking place on Earth. They are people who had turned to
Christ in the midst of the worst circumstances that had ever existed
on Earth. Satan and the antichrist are in charge and are fighting God
with everything they have.

He will defy God and exalt himself over everything
that is adored. He will set himself up in God's
Temple, claiming to be God. (2 Thessalonians 2:4)

The antichrist is persecuting and killing every Israelite and every
follower of Jesus Christ that he can identify. To proclaim the Lord
under these circumstances will take tremendous courage, because it
will mean almost certain death. The conviction and courage of these
mortals in turning to God will be incredible, and yet they will do
that—by the thousands and thousands.

These martyrs will never again be hungry or thirsty. Jesus Christ
has given them the water of life.

On the last day of Passover, Jesus declared to the
crowds, "If anyone is thirsty, come to Me and
drink. The Scriptures declare that streams of living water will flow from anyone who believes in
Me." He was speaking of the Holy Spirit who
would be given to everyone believing in Him.
(John 7:37–39)

The Holy Spirit probably will not remain on Earth after the
Rapture. Therefore, it is even more incredible that those who turn to
Jesus Christ will be able to endure without the support of the Holy

Spirit, who lives within us Christians during the church age and who holds Satan back.

> The work this man of rebellion and hell will do when he comes is already happening, but he will not come until the one who is holding him back steps out of the way. (2 Thessalonians 2:7)

The Lamb of God will be their Shepherd.

> The Lord is my Shepherd. I shall not want. He makes me lie down in green pastures. He leads me to waters. He restores my soul. He leads me in His righteousness. (Psalm 23:1–3)

CHAPTER 8

Revelation 8:1–13

The sun will be turned to darkness and the moon to blood before
the dreadful Day of the Lord shall come. Everyone who calls upon
the Name of the Lord will be saved. Even on Mt. Zion those
He has called will be delivered, just as the Lord has promised.

—Joel 2:31–32

REVELATION 8:1–5. The Lamb breaks the
seventh seal on the scroll, and there is absolute
silence in Heaven for half an hour. Seven angels
stand before the Throne of God, and they are
each given a trumpet. Another angel stands before
the Altar holding a censer. He receives incense
to mix with the prayers of God's people, and he
offers this up on the golden Altar. The aroma of
the prayers and incense begin to ascend to God.
Then the angel fills the golden censer with fire
from the Altar and hurls it on the Earth. There
are rumbles of thunder and flashes of lightning,
and a great earthquake.

Finally, the Lamb breaks the seventh seal on the scroll. Now the
scroll is completely open. However, this seventh seal is not a
final judgment—it opens up another series of increasingly severe
judgments. The worst is still to come! There is profound silence in

heaven. The choir of millions stops singing. Heaven holds its breath for half an hour. In the profound silence in heaven, the prayers of the suffering saints on Earth are heard. The silence is broken as the prayers reach the throne of God. Another angel is holding a golden censer filled with coals from the altar. He is given the sweet aroma of the prayers of God's people on Earth to mix with the incense and warm coals in the censer.

What is the scroll that is held by the "Lamb who was slain before the creation of the world" (Revelation 13:8)? God is all-knowing, and He knew the outcome when He gave us the freedom to choose. He knew we would sin. He knew that some of us would reject Him. He knew that some of us would love Him. He knew that some would sit on the fence until we are forced to make a decision. He knew that there would have to be a reckoning.

> O Lord, I will praise Your Name. You planned wonderful things long ago, and they have come to be just as You said. Mighty cities become ruins and strong forts are rubble. Palaces disappear, never to be rebuilt. Strong and ruthless Nations shake with fear and glorify Your Name. But to the poor, You are a refuge from the storm, a protection from the heat, and a shelter from merciless men. (Isaiah 25:1–4)

The scroll is God's plan for the final reckoning. It is the plan for judgments that will be poured out on the antichrist and his followers on Earth during Daniel's seventieth week (Daniel 9:26–27). After the Rapture of the church, there will be a power vacuum, which opens the way for a takeover by the antichrist.

Remember, the antichrist rode out on a white horse carrying a weapon (his credentials) when the Lamb opened the first seal (Revelation 6:1–2). The antichrist will assume leadership of the European Union. One of his first acts will be to make a treaty with Israel, which will be broken (Revelation 12:6). Under his leadership, the Earth will become more and more violent. The red horse of anarchy is running amok (Revelation 6:4).

Many people will come down from the fence and embrace the antichrist, enamored by his power and deception, and by his rhetoric. Don't we love rhetoric! But many people will come down from the fence to embrace God and the Lamb. It will be very difficult for them, because Satan and the antichrist will come against them with vengeance.

Another angel is holding a censer or container filled with coals from the altar. He is given the sweet aroma of the prayers of God's people on Earth to mix with the incense and the warm coals in the censer. In the profound silence in heaven, the prayers of the suffering saints on Earth are heard loud and clear. The silence is broken as the prayers of those people on Earth who have learned to love the Lord reach the ears of God in heaven.

The angel fills the censer with fire from the altar and throws it down to the Earth, causing a great storm. We see lightning, and we hear thunder and the sound of a great earthquake.

> REVELATION 8:6–12. The seven angels lift their trumpets. Then the first angel blows his trumpet and fire and hail and blood fall upon the Earth. The fire consumes a third of the Earth, burning trees and the green grass. When the second angel blows his trumpet, a blazing mountain falls into the sea. A third of all the ships are immediately destroyed, a third of the creatures of the sea are killed, and the sea turns bloody red. The third angel sounds his trumpet and a blazing star named Wormwood falls from the sky and a third of the rivers and freshwater turns bitter and many people are poisoned. The fourth angel sounds his trumpet and a third of the sun and of the moon and of the stars turn dark. A third of the day and a third of the night become dark.

The judgment unleashed by the first trumpet is probably built upon global warming. A third of the land is simply burned up. More than a century of increased carbon release from smokestacks and exhausts has taken a toll on the Earth's climate and vegetation. Prolonged lack of rainfall has made Earth's plant life fragile, like fuel waiting for a spark. The sounding of this trumpet brings fires that consume a third of the Earth.

Although the Revelation of Jesus Christ is primarily a picture of God's judgment upon the New Roman Empire (Daniel 7:8), global warming is worldwide. The effects of increased global temperature is felt today. The campfire that burned Paradise, California, to the ground in November 2018 was just a precursor of what is to come. It was the sixth deadliest wildfire ever experienced in the United States, but the whole world is fast becoming a tinderbox.

The increased temperature is melting the icecaps and glaciers, which will exacerbate the global warming. Sea levels are rising, and coastlines will change. Ports and harbors and low-lying terrain are submerging. All this is changing the habitats of man and beast, and is disrupting food supplies. We have been warned for years, and yet seemingly intelligent people choose not to believe. We are told that a fourth of the world will be destroyed by war, famine, disease, and wild animals (Revelation 6:7–8). We are increasingly facing Lyme disease because of displaced insects. We are even facing red algae blooms. Prior to the release of the children of Israel from Egyptian slavery, God warned Pharaoh repeatedly to, "Let My People Go!" God told Moses,

> If they don't accept the first miracle, take water
> from the Nile River and pour it upon the dry
> land. It will turn to blood. (Exodus 4:9)

Global warming is causing saltwater blooms of toxic red algae. An emergency situation was declared in Florida in 2017. Freshwater red algae is also increasing in Lake Erie. At the turn of the AD second century, John has no words to pinpoint this plague, so he calls the red waters "blood."

We have refugees fleeing war and hunger and oppression world-wide. It is a sign of the times that Christian countries are refusing to offer refuge to the suffering poor and oppressed, even though God sets that example for us.

> But to the poor, You are a refuge from the storm,
> a protection from the heat, and a shelter from
> merciless men. (Isaiah 25:4)

In World War II, Germany oppressed the children of Israel. God's wife (Hosea 2:14–16) was oppressed, imprisoned, and subjected to the most inhuman atrocities. Millions of God's beloved were killed by starvation and in gas chambers. After the end of the "war to end all wars," the thoughtful people of the world suffered great remorse. When modern countries began refusing to take in refugees in the early twenty-first century, Germany's prime minister, Angela Merkel, refused to fall into that trap. The painful memories of Germany's history helped her to take a humanitarian stance, but most of the world has a very short memory. If we don't learn from past mistakes, we are doomed to repeat those mistakes.

In the end, God will judge the merciless men. As vegetation decreases and habitats are destroyed, hungry wild animals will forage for food, and we will become that food. Humans will become the hunted. Will we pray for forgiveness for our blind self-absorption?

The second trumpet blast affects the Mediterranean Sea. John sees a blazing mountain fall into the sea This may be a real mountain. Mount Etna in Sicily is slipping into the sea. It is moving very slowly, but the primary force causing the slippage is gravity. The pull of gravity is moving the mountain from its more elevated position toward the lower elevation of the Ionian Sea. An additional force contributing to this movement is the shift of weight when magma flows upward in the recesses of the mountain above sea level. Structural weaknesses, including fault lines caused by seismic activity, adds to the slippage.

Will the blast from the second trumpet be the force which impels the mountain into the sea? Huge billows of smoke and plumes of steam will fill the air when a fiery mountain falls into the sea. People live on the mountain. A huge tsunami will destroy the coastal lands around the entire Mediterranean Sea. Ships will capsize, and sea creatures will die. Blood will literally color the waters of the Mediterranean. Rotting carrion will wash ashore all around the sea, and the stench will be unbearable. Disease will explode. The pale horse of Death will be out of control and Hades follows close behind. A fourth of the Earth will die (Revelation 6:7–8).

The third trumpet judgment is against the fresh waters, which are vital to the survival of mankind. An asteroid named Wormwood plunges to the Earth. Another name for the plant artemisia is wormwood. Artemisia has a licorice taste and was used in making absinthe, which was outlawed because it was a narcotic poison.

The effects of the asteroid Wormwood will be bitterly unpleasant and grievous. It will destroy and pollute a third of the drinking water. We need about a dozen cups of liquid per day, including liquid in our food. But Wormwood will also destroy the water we use in food preparation. People will literally die of thirst. Our bodies are at least 60 percent water, and we have to sustain that level. The vulnerable can only survive about three days without water. Without water, healthy people can only survive about a week. The United Nations has established that drinking water of a quality and in quantities to meet their basic needs is a basic human right. This is a right that is being denied to many refugees. The result of global warming and attendant wildfires mean less water and, when it hits, Wormwood will deny necessary water to a third of the population.

The fourth trumpet is sounded, and the world grows even darker. The ash and smoke and toxins released by the plunging of the mountain into the sea take their toll. The crashing of Wormwood into the Earth sends more plumes of smoke and dust and debris into the atmosphere. There is less daylight, and the nights are darker. The air is so polluted that people can hardly breathe. People everywhere are wearing masks. Babies die. The elderly die. Even the fittest humans die. A single eagle is seen flying overhead.

Confess your sins and pray for each other so that you may be healed. The prayer of a righteous man is powerful and effective. (James 5:16)

REVELATION 8:13. An eagle flies overhead calling, "Woe! Woe to the people on Earth. Woe, because of the trumpet blasts to come.

CHAPTER 9

Revelation 9:1–21

O Lucifer, son of the morning! How you are fallen from Heaven. You were mighty against the nations, but you said to yourself, "I will ascend to Heaven and rule the angels. I will take the highest throne and preside on the Mount of Assembly. I will ascend above the clouds and be like the Most High." You will be brought down to the pit.

—Isaiah 14:12–15

REVELATION 9:1–11. The Fifth Angel blows his trumpet, and a star falls from the sky to the Earth carrying the keys to the bottomless pit. When he opens it, smoke pours out, further darkening the sun. Locusts come flying out of the smoke and descend to the ground. They cannot attack those who have the Seal of God or damage the vegetation. They have the power to attack the people who do not have the Seal of God for five months. They have tails that sting like scorpions and the people are in agony and want to die, but they cannot end their agony. These locusts look like little horses in battle armor, but they have faces like men, and hair like women. They have strong breastplates, and gold crowns, and when they swarm their wings sound like chariots rushing to battle. These locusts are the subjects of Apollyon, or Abaddon, or the Destroyer, the Prince of the Bottomless Pit. This is the first woe.

Who or what is this being who descends to the Earth like a falling star? Some people think that it is an angel. Some have even postulated that it is Jesus Christ executing judgment. No, it is Satan! And he is carrying the keys to the bottomless pit. He will release his legions! For all these eons, Satan has been in heaven accusing the people before God, but he has now been expelled.

> There was war in Heaven and Michael and the angels under his command fought the Dragon and his fallen angels. The Dragon lost the battle and was forced from Heaven. The Dragon is the ancient serpent called the Devil or Satan. He has deceived the whole world, but he is thrown down to the Earth with all his army. (Revelation 12:7–9)

Did demons roam the Earth prior to the first coming of Jesus Christ? During His ministry on Earth, the Lord expelled demons from many people. Since the fulfillment of the Feast of Passover or Shavuot (Leviticus 23:15–22) and the arrival of the Holy Spirit to indwell Christians, have these demons been restrained?

> "What is your name?" Jesus asked the demon who had taken control of the man. "Legion," was the reply. The man was filled with thousands of them. They begged Jesus not to order them into the Bottomless Pit, but to allow them to enter a herd of pigs. They left the man and entered the pigs. Immediately the whole herd rushed down the mountain and fell over a cliff into a lake and drowned. (Luke 8:30–33)

If the Holy Spirit has restrained Satan's demons while He has indwelled Christians during the church age, will they be released if the Holy Spirit returns to heaven along with the Christians at the Rapture? Satan has the keys to the bottomless pit where the demons are restrained. When Satan opens the pit, enough smoke pours out to darken the sun. A vast number of his demons swarm out with the smoke. They look somewhat like locusts, but they have tails like scorpions, and they resemble little horses with men's faces.

This first woe lasts for five months. The woes are waves of warfare, hardship, and destruction.

> REVELATION 9:12–21. The Sixth Angel blows his trumpet and we hear a voice coming from the four horns of the Altar commanding this angel to release the four fallen angels held at the River Euphrates. When they are freed, they muster an army of 200 million warriors, empowered to kill a third of all the people on earth. Most of the warriors are wearing red breastplates, but some wear sky blue or yellow. The mounts have heads like lions. Fire and sulfur billow out from their mouths, and their tails look like serpents. As we watch, a third of all mankind is killed. But the people remaining on Earth still refuse to repent or to worship God, clinging to their idols and immorality.

The Lamb commands the sixth angel to release four fallen angels who are being held at the Euphrates River, bordering Iraq. The lines are being drawn. These fallen angels stir armies who have been waiting. They will lead them into battle. During the impending battle, a third of the Earth's remaining population will be killed. Who are they going to fight against? They will fight against God's people!

Jesus revealed these scenes to John probably around AD 90. John's experiences were first century, but he was seeing things which some two thousand years later are still impending. He did not have the technical information or the language—he just had the assignment. He did a remarkable job when he described these strange things. What John saw was twenty-first-century machines of war, but he was living in the Iron Age—daunting! John was seeing airplanes, helicopters, machine guns, and army tanks. John saw the New Roman Empire—the European Union—poised for battle. This saga will end where it began. The rest of the world is "the islands," which disappear and will not be found (Revelation 16:20).

In the face of all this carnage, the population still clings to their idols. What are the idols of our modern age? What are the things we hold dear? We love our fine houses and our fancy cars. We love our clothes and our money and our social media. Would we put our phones down? Or would we turn to the internet for information rather than turn to God?

John gives us a glimpse of the players in the unfolding events. Following the great flood, the sons of Noah moved out into the world. Ham's family settled in Egypt, around the Mediterranean, in Europe, and eastward to Iraq and Iran. Japheth's family moved north into Russia and in the Ukraine. Shem's family, the messianic line, continued to live in the Middle East and spread eastward.

Red is the color associated with Russia, and the red breastplates indicate that Japheth's descendants are leading this global battle of end-times. The blue breastplates are from the European Union and indicate that Ham's descendants are joining in the fray. Yellow is the color of the Vatican's flag. Remember, the Christians who occupy the Vatican will vacate it and fly to heaven at the Rapture. When Christians vacate the Vatican, the false prophet (Revelation 13:11–15) will appropriate it and just move in.

CHAPTER 10

Revelation 10:1–11

My heart pounds and leaps within me. Listen to the roar of
God's voice as it comes from His mouth. Lightening is unleashed
to the ends of the Earth as His voice rolls across Heaven. Hear
the thunder of His majestic voice. God's voice is glorious
and we cannot comprehend the greatness of His power.

—Job 37:1–5

REVELATION 10:1–7. A mighty angel leaves
Heaven, and descends to Earth wrapped in a
cloud, and a rainbow gleams above his head. His
face shines like the sun, and his feet are like fire.
He is carrying a small scroll. When he stands on
the Earth with his right foot on the sea and his
left foot on the land, he roars like a lion. Seven
thunders crash in reply but I am instructed not
to write down the words. The mighty angel raises
his right hand and invokes the Name of God,
declaring that there should be no further delay.
The Seventh Angel prepares to blow his trumpet. God's mysterious plan which has been proclaimed through the ages by His prophets, will
be fulfilled.

Many people associate this great angel with the Lord Jesus Christ, but this is an angel. Jesus Christ, the Lamb of God, is in heaven, and He will not return to the Earth until His second coming—not even for the Rapture. When it is time for the Tribulation to begin, Jesus will step out of heaven and call us with the sound of a trumpet. We will leave the Earth and meet Jesus in the air (1 Thessalonians 4:16–18).

This being who floats to the Earth from heaven in a cloud is a truly awesome angel! He can stand with one foot on the land and the other foot on the sea. His face is shining like the sun—He has been in the presence of God. His feet are like fire. Can you imagine a sailor on a ship on the Mediterranean Sea staring at this huge fiery foot standing on (not in) the water?

This mighty angel's voice sounds like the roar of a lion. When he roars, he is answered by seven thunders. The thunders are the voice of God responding to or giving instructions to this mighty angel. This book of the Revelation of Jesus Christ is an unsealing of the future, but here we have an enigma, John is told *not* to write down God's words. God's response is still sealed up today. We have a great mystery. Why would God seal up a portion of this great revealing?

Was this the angel who asked, "Who is worthy to unseal the scroll" (Revelation 5:2)? This is a relevant question, because this angel is also holding a small open scroll. The angel raises his right hand and declares in the name of God that there will be no further delay. The judgments proclaimed by the prophets down through the ages will now be fulfilled.

> Don't forget dear friends, a day is like a thousand years, and a thousand years is like tomorrow with the Lord. He is not slow about His promised return, but He is patient and waiting for sinners to repent, because He is not willing that any of us should perish. (2 Peter 3:8–9)

God has been patient down through the ages, not willing to abandon any of us, but God's patience must yield to God's justice.

The time has come for the inhabitants on Earth to make a choice between God and Satan. The time has come for Satan to be banished. The time has come for Jesus Christ to reign for one thousand years.

The seventh angel prepares to blow his trumpet.

> REVELATION 10:8–11. The voice from Heaven now tells me, John, to go down and get the scroll which the mighty angel is holding. I descend to the Earth and ask the angel for the scroll. He hands the scroll to me with instructions to eat it. "It will taste like honey in your mouth, but it will sour in your stomach." I eat the scroll, and as my stomach is churning, the angel tells me that I must prophesy about the things I see.

John is told to take the scroll from the angel, to consume it, and then to prophesy. He leaves heaven and goes to the angel. The angel gives the scroll to John with instructions to eat it, but he warns that this scroll will upset John's stomach.

This is not the only time in Scripture that someone is told to eat a scroll. While the Israelites were in exile in Babylon, God sent Ezekiel to speak to them. Just as God gave His Word to Ezekiel to speak, He is giving John His Word to speak to those who suffer during the Tribulation. Just as Ezekiel was told to warn the exiles in Babylon, God is warning these Tribulation exiles that this is their last chance.

> "You must speak My Word to the Israelites, whether they listen or not. Remember, they are rebellious. Son of man, do not be a rebel, but listen to what I say. Open your mouth and eat what I give you." I saw a hand holding out a scroll which was unrolled. Words of mourning and woe were written on both sides. "Son of man, eat this scroll and then go and speak its message to

the people of Israel." He gave me the scroll and I ate it, and it tasted as sweet as honey. (Ezekiel 2:7–3:3)

Are these accounts literal or figurative? Did John and Ezekiel really eat the scrolls, or did they consume them? Did they study God's words and commit them to memory so that they could deliver God's message? There is another passage in which Jeremiah seems to have consumed God's Word.

When Your Words came, I ate them. They are food for my hungry soul. They bring joy to my heart and delight me. I am proud to bear Your Name, O Lord. (Jeremiah 15:16)

Scrolls were usually made of sheepskin and were rolled on pieces of wood. That would be very difficult to chew up and swallow. These passages seem to be accounts of visions. However, He accomplished it, God implanted His words in the hearts and minds of His messenger. And Jeremiah, Ezekiel, and John were all faithful to deliver His message to His people.

God's laws are perfect. They protect us and make us wise. They give us joy and light. God's laws are pure and just and eternal, and they are more desirable than gold. They are sweeter than honey because they give success to those who obey them. (Psalm 19:7–11)

CHAPTER 11

Revelation 11:1–19

For this will be the days of God's judgment. The words of the ancient Scriptures written by the prophets will be fulfilled.

—Luke 21:22

REVELATION 11:1–6. I, John, am handed a measuring rod and instructed to measure the Temple, including the inner court where the Altar stands, and to count the worshipers. "But do not to measure the outer court of the Temple, because it is given over to the Nations who will trample Jerusalem for 42 months. I will give power to My two witnesses who are clothed in sackcloth to prophesy for 1260 days. Anyone who tries to harm these two witnesses will be consumed by fire coming from their mouths. They are the two olive trees and lampstands standing before the Lord. My prophets have the power to withhold rain from the Earth for the duration of their prophesy, to turn the waters to blood, and to send plagues upon the people."

Up to this point, the antichrist has been establishing his control over the whole world and solidifying the support of his followers. Things have gone fairly smoothly, and even though world conditions are unravelling because of global warming, food and water shortages, and cataclysmic events, he is popular. Chapters 11 and 12 set the stage for the second half of the Tribulation—the Great Tribulation. The worst is yet to come. There are 1,260 days remaining.

While John was down on Earth eating the small scroll held by the mighty angel, he was given a backbreaking task. The temple has been built, perhaps under an agreement between the Israelites and the antichrist. John was given something like a yardstick and was told to measure the temple except for the outer court. Why would he be instructed to count the people in the temple? Because they are God's faithful. They are children of Israel who are not a part of the rabble in the outer court—they have not embraced the antichrist. They are the ones who God will protect during the second half of the Tribulation (Daniel 9:26–27).

The Israelite calendar was made up of thirty-day months. The time periods set out in the Revelation are based on thirty-day months. Therefore, 1,260 days is the same as 42 months and is the same as 3 1/2 years. John is told not to measure the outer court because it will be under the control of the nations—the Gentiles—for the second half of the Tribulation. These 3 1/2 years are in the first half of the Tribulation. Soon the antichrist will set up the abomination of desolation in the temple (Daniel 11:31; Matthew 24:15), and the Israelites will flee.

During the ensuing 42 months, God's two witnesses will be in the outer court prophesying with God's protection, and then God will take them home. These two witnesses are clothed in sackcloth—a garment of mourning, and they call upon the crowds to repent. They have special powers. If anyone tries to harm them, they only have to open their mouths and fire will emerge and consume the enemy. They can bring plagues, or illness, upon their enemies, and they can turn water to blood, resulting in a lot of extreme thirst.

These two prophets are probably Enoch (Genesis 22:24) and Elijah (2 Kings 2:11), since neither of them tasted death. They were transported to heaven by God. God says they are the two olive trees and menorah standing before Him (Zechariah 4:3). The Holy Spirit will undoubtedly be with these two prophets, supporting them and their ministry.

Inside the temple is the court of the women, the court of the priests, and the holy of holies. The golden altar is in the court of the priests. Outside is the court of the Gentiles, where God's two witnesses prophesy during the Great Tribulation.

> REVELATION 11:7–14. Upon completion of the 3 1/2 years of their prophesy, the Destroyer who was freed from the bottomless pit kills them. Their dead bodies lay exposed for 3 1/2 days in Jerusalem where Jesus Christ was crucified. Ungodly people all over the Earth declare a holiday and exchange gifts, celebrating the death of the prophets whose words have tormented them. After 3 1/2 days The Holy Spirit enters them, they stand up, and a loud voice from Heaven shouts, "Come up!" They ascend to Heaven. A great earthquake levels a tenth of Jerusalem, and 7,000 people are killed. The ungodly people are filled with terror, and they acknowledge God's hand. This is the second woe.

When Satan is thrown out of heaven, he will release the destroyer from the bottomless pit (Revelation 9:1–11). At the conclusion of three and a half years of ministry, the destroyer will kill the two witnesses. The bodies of the two witnesses will not be buried, but they will lay in the courtyard for three and a half days. The followers of the antichrist will celebrate their deaths. They will even exchange gifts. This celebration will be like a false Easter, marking the death, resurrection, and ascension of the prophets, because after three and a half days, the Holy Spirit will breathe life into His prophets and they will stand up. Everyone will be engulfed in fear. A loud voice from heaven will shout, "Come up!" Their enemies will watch them ascend into heaven in a cloud.

Everyone will instantly be able to see exactly what is happening, because of modern social media, television, computers, and phones.

This is the end of the second woe.

REVELATION 11:15–19. Immediately the Seventh Angel blows his trumpet and the people on Earth hear shouts from Heaven. "The world is the Kingdom of God and of Christ. He shall reign forever." The 24 Elders fall down and worship God. "We give thanks to Lord God Almighty. You have asserted your power and have begun to reign. The Nations rebelled against you, but it is now time to judge the dead and to reward your prophets." The Temple in Heaven opens and I see the Ark of His Covenant inside. On Earth, there is lightning, and thunder, a great hailstorm, and an earthquake.

The blowing of the seventh trumpet sets the stage for the onset of the third woe. John has returned to heaven. Everyone in heaven is celebrating the end, but the celebration is premature. There is unfinished business on Earth. The heavenly inhabitants love God and always worship Him. The elders intone, "You have begun to reign." But God has never left His throne. Heaven's temple opens, and John gets a glimpse of the ark of the covenant. The ark is like a wooden cedar chest covered with gold. A pot of manna, Aaron's rod, and the Ten Commandments on slabs of stone are stored inside the ark, remnants from the forty years the children of Israel spent wandering in the desert. The mercy seat is on the top, surrounded by two cherubim facing each other (Exodus 25:10–22).

Things are bad down on Earth. There is lightning, thunder, and hail. Weather patterns have worsened dramatically since the turn of the twenty-first century due to global warming. Weather patterns are more erratic as a result of the melting of the ice caps and increased surface temperature. Changing weather patterns have brought on increased droughts. Precipitation may occur in unusual places and may be unusually heavy because warmer air can hold more water vapor. Then there is a great earthquake!

CHAPTER 12

Revelation 12:1–16

Then Daniel saw two men on the banks of a river. One asked the Man in linen robes, "How long will it be until all these terrors end?" Lifting His hands to Heaven and swearing by the eternal God, He replied, "They will not end until a time and times and half a time [3 1/2 years] after the power of God's people has been crushed."

—Daniel 12:5–7

REVELATION 12:1–6. A great sign appears in Heaven. I see a pregnant woman dressed like the sun, with the moon beneath her feet, and wearing a crown of 12 stars. She cries out with labor pains. A red Dragon with seven crowned heads and ten horns stands before her, ready to eat her child. The Dragon is Satan. A flip of the Dragon's tail dashes stars down to the Earth. The woman delivers a Son Who will rule the Nations with an iron hand, and the Child is swept up to God.

This brings to mind a dream which Jacob's son Joseph had when he was a boy nearly four thousand years ago. He was the eleventh of Jacob's twelve sons and the firstborn of Jacob's beloved Rachel. Jacob doted on Joseph, and his older brothers resented it. Joseph had a dream which he recounted to his brothers, and it angered them.

He had another dream and told his father and his brothers, "Listen to my dream. The sun, moon, and eleven stars bowed down before me!" Jacob rebuked him, "Shall your mother and brothers and I bow before you?" His brothers were angry, but Jacob pondered what it meant. (Genesis 37:9–11)

Jacob had insight into the ways of God. He recognized that the dream was about his own family: Jacob was the sun, Rachel was the moon, and Joseph's eleven brothers were the stars, all bowing down to his twelfth son. God loves to give His people special names, and "Israel" was His special name for Jacob. Jacob's twelve sons were the foundations of the twelve tribes of Israel.

God said to him, "You shall no longer be called Jacob, but Israel. I Am God Almighty, and I will multiply you. You will become a great Nation, and many Nations and many kings will descend from you. I will give the Land I gave to Abraham and Isaac to you and your descendants." (Genesis 35:10–12)

We recognize that the woman in Revelation 12 is a depiction of the nation Israel. Jacob's line was the messianic line, and Satan was desperate to stymie God's plan for the redemption of humankind. But Satan was not successful and Jesus Christ, our Redeemer, was born. Satan tried to destroy the baby Messiah shortly after His birth. Working through King Herod, Satan killed all the baby boys in Bethlehem.

After the wise men were gone, an angel appeared to Joseph in a dream. "King Herod will try to kill the Child. Take the Baby and Mary and flee to Egypt. Stay there until I tell you to return." Joseph left for Egypt with Mary and the Child

> that night… Herod sent soldiers to Bethlehem
> with orders to kill every baby boy two years of age
> and younger. (Matthew 2:13–16)

The Messiah had to be born a human so that He could die for our sins, but His death was on God's terms. Satan was unsuccessful in his efforts to destroy our Redeemer, even though he continued even while Christ was on the cross. Christ only lived about thirty years and then He was "swept up to God." Jesus Christ died, was resurrected, and He returned to heaven. When He returns to Earth for His millennial reign, He will "rule the nations with a heavy hand."

Through the ages, Satan has been in heaven standing before God and accusing God's people, but that is about to change. The depiction of Satan as the red dragon with ten horns on seven crowned heads tells us that there will be ten principal nations heading up the European Union, but only seven of them will exert power (Revelation 13:1–2).

At the onset of the Tribulation, the European Union (the New Roman Empire, Daniel 7:8) is the world government headed up by the antichrist. Another player, the false prophet (Revelation 13:1–8), is their accomplice. He moves into the Vatican after the Rapture of Christians. Satan will seek to accomplish his work through them and the nations. Meet the unholy trinity. After the Rapture of Christians to heaven (1 Thessalonians 4:16–17), the only people of God living on Earth are the children of Israel and people who turn to Jesus Christ after the Rapture.

Satan's expulsion from heaven halfway through the Tribulation is imminent, and many angels (stars) will fall with him. Unsuccessful in his efforts to destroy her baby, Satan will pursue Israel, and she will flee from the holy land into the wilderness, where God will protect her for the remaining 3 1/2 years of the Tribulation. Many people speculate that God will shelter the Israelis in the ancient city of Petra in Jordan.

> Then in Heaven the mighty angelic prince
> Michael, who guards over Israel, will fight for
> you against Satan's forces. There will be a time of

anguish for Israel greater than any previous suffering, but everyone whose names are written in the Book will endure. (Daniel 12:1)

REVELATION 12:7–12. War breaks out in Heaven. The Archangel Michael and his angels fight Satan the Dragon and his troop of angels. The Dragon is overcome, and a loud voice announces that the Kingdom of God and Christ has come, and that the Accuser of God's people has been defeated by the blood of the Lamb. Satan has been thrown from Heaven down to the Earth. "Woe to the people of the world because the Devil knows his time is short, and he is angry."

Although it has not happened yet, the prophet Isaiah saw Satan's fall some 2,700 years ago.

O Lucifer, you have fallen from Heaven. You who weakened the Nations are cut to the ground because you said in your heart that you would raise your throne above the stars of God. You said you would ascend above the clouds and place your throne on the sacred mountain and be like the Most High. (Isaiah 14:12–15)

The third woe has begun. Satan is called "the Accuser of God's people" (Job 1:6–7). Now God is ready to force the people remaining on Earth to either turn to Him or perish with the evil. The elders have already begun to praise God for ending Satan's rebellion (Revelation 11:16–18). The archangel Michael and God's angels make a stand against Satan and the angels who have chosen to follow him (Revelation 12:4). The Great Tribulation has begun. Satan and his forces are now down on Earth, tormenting and killing God's people. This is called the time of Jacob's trouble.

Alas, when has there ever been such a time of terror? It is a time of trouble for My people such as has never been known before. Yet God will rescue them! (Jeremiah 30:7)

REVELATION 12:13–16. On Earth, the Dragon persecutes the woman, but she is given wings to fly into the wilderness to a place where God will protect her for the remaining time and times and half a time [3 1/2 years] of the Tribulation. We are shaken as Satan attempts to destroy the woman with a great flood of water, but the Earth swallows up the flood. Unable to destroy the Israelites, Satan attacks the Christians who belong to Jesus.

God promised that He would give Israel wings so she could escape Satan's persecution. He had made this promise to Israel before. He delivered assurance to His people through the prophet Isaiah during the time of King Hezekiah.

O Jacob, you say the Lord doesn't see your troubles. Don't you know yet that the everlasting God never grows weary? He gives power to the tired and strength to the weak. Your young men will be exhausted, but the Lord shall renew the strength of those who wait upon Him. They shall fly with the wings of eagles. They shall run and not be weary. (Isaiah 40:27–31)

Because of God's protection, the children of Israel will be able to escape the murderous hand of Satan for 3 1/2 years. Satan is pictured as attempting to destroy Israel "with a great flood of water." This does not indicate that Satan will try to drown the Israelites. This is a reference to vast armies coming against God's people. God made a similar analogy to Isaiah.

> Since the people of Jerusalem refuse the gently flowing waters of Shiloah, but rely on King Rezin and King Pekah to aid them, I will overwhelm them with floodwaters of the Euphrates. The king of Assyria and his mighty army will overflow their banks and swirl over them up to their necks. Assyria will sweep into Judah and submerge you. (Isaiah 8:6–8)

God promises that Satan's flood of armies will not destroy the Israelites, but that the Earth will swallow the "flood." It will not be the first time that the Earth has swallowed the enemy of God's people. When the children of Israel were wandering in the wilderness, some of the group rebelled against Moses.

> Moses told the Children of Israel that if the Lord opened up the ground and swallowed the tents of the rebellious Korah, Dathan, and Abiram, they would know that these men despised God. He had hardly finished speaking when the ground suddenly split beneath them and swallowed them, their tents, their families and their friends. They went down alive into Sheol and the Earth closed over them. (Numbers 6:30–33)

CHAPTER 13

Revelation 13:1–18

But if you are unwilling to obey the Lord, then decide today whom you will obey...But as for me and my family, we will serve the Lord.

—Joshua 24:15

> REVELATION 13:1–4. I see a strange Beast which had seven heads and 10 horns wearing crowns rising up out of the sea. Blasphemous names insulting God were written on each head. It looked like a leopard, with a lion's mouth and a bear's feet. The Dragon gives the Beast his own power and authority and throne. One of the heads has a fatal wound, but the wound is healed. The people are in awe and worship the Beast and the Dragon for giving him such power. "Who is able to fight against him?"

John sees a strange beast rising out of the sea. The beast looked like a leopard (Daniel 7:6), which is the symbol of the Greek Empire. The beast had a lion's mouth (Daniel 7:4), which is the symbol of the Babylonian Empire (Iraq). But the beast also has the feet of a bear (Daniel 7:5), which is a symbol of the Persian Empire (Iran). Even though the revelation is about the conclusion of the Roman Empire (Daniel 7:7–8), these other empires were precursors and continue to exert influence in the modern world. The Romans briefly conquered

Iraq and parts of Iran, but they did not hold much influence over those countries. However, these countries continue to interact with and affect the European Union. Recently, Iran has partially withdrawn from a nuclear agreement with the European Union. The beast is the final empire—the New Roman Empire.

The time of the Gentiles began when Babylon conquered Jerusalem in 597 BC (Daniel 9). All the empires have been Gentile. Also, the Christian era began with the death of the Anointed One (Jesus Christ) and will continue until the Rapture preceding the rise of the antichrist. The antichrist will reign for seven years. At the end of the seven years, Jesus Christ will return to begin His millennial reign.

The strange beast that John saw rising from the sea is the antichrist, the leader of the New Roman Empire—the European Union. He will be the final Gentile leader. His rising out of the sea means that the antichrist will be a popular leader. The reign of the beast will be synonymous with the New Roman Empire (Daniel 7:7–9). Satan, the antichrist, and the New Roman Empire all have the same description—seven heads with ten horns. One of the heads has been killed and "healed." It would have been healed by the dragon, who assumed control and gave him satanic powers.

Some 2,600 years ago, the Lord gave Daniel insight into this puzzle that we are now confronting in the AD twenty-first century.

> This fourth beast is the fourth world power which will rule the Earth [Rome]. It will be more brutal than any of the others and it will devour and destroy the whole world. Its 10 horns are 10 kings [countries] that will rise out of this empire. Then another more brutal king [Antichrist] will destroy three of them. He will defy Almighty God and wear down the saints with persecution. He will try to change the laws, morals, and customs, and God's people will be helpless in his hands for 3 1/2 years. (Daniel 7:23–25)

The revelation of Jesus Christ is all about the final empire—the New Roman Empire. The Roman Empire was the fourth in the succession of Babylon, Persia, Greece, and Rome, which were revealed to the prophet, Daniel some 2,600 years ago. There has always been a quest for world domination among ruthless leaders down through the ages. So far, no one has achieved that goal, but during the Tribulation, the antichrist and the New Roman Empire will attain that goal.

The Roman Empire conquered Europe. However, the Roman Empire itself was never conquered. It survived numerous internal wars and has continued down through the centuries in a somewhat disintegrated form, but Europe has mostly continued to use the Roman civil code as its basic law (Justinian institutions).

Then the European Union was founded on November 1, 1993. It is headquartered in Brussels, Belgium, and its parliament building which is located in Strasbourg, France, is modeled after the Tower of Babel (Revelation 18:2–3). Will the antichrist set up his headquarters in Rome? Images of Europa (Greek goddess of the moon) riding Zeus (Greek god of the sky) are on its stamps and coins (Revelation 17:3–5). Its flag features twelve gold stars on a blue background (Revelation 9:16–18). Is this setting the stage for Daniel's final king (Daniel 7:24)? This final king will uproot three of the ten horns (Daniel 7:8). Is Brexit a part of this prophecy?

The red dragon (Revelation 12:3–4) is Satan. Notice that he also has seven heads and has ten horns. Trying to make himself like God, he has molded the final horrible world society and its world leader in his own image. They are inseparable. Remember, Christians are in heaven (1 Thessalonians 4:15–17), and they are with God the Father, God the Son, and God the Holy Spirit. But through the Tribulation, God has people who He loves down on the Earth. Some people who remain on Earth following the Rapture turn to Jesus Christ, and the children of Israel also remain on Earth through these horrible seven years. This will be the reality of dystopia. We have reached the halfway mark. The beast (antichrist) was killed, and his body is indwelled by Satan—the "false resurrection."

REVELATION 13:5–10. The Dragon encourages the Beast to blaspheme God and His Temple, and he gives the Beast power over the Earth for 42 months [3 1/2 years]. The Beast has the power to rule over all mankind and to overcome God's people. Anyone whose name is not written in the Book of Life will worship the Beast. He who has an ear, listen. God's people will be arrested and killed. Be faithful and endure.

Remember, Jesus warned us two thousand years ago:

> Nations will rise against each other. There will be famines and earthquakes, but this will only be the beginning of the horrors. You will be hated and persecuted and killed because of Me. Many of you turn away from faith and will betray and hate each other. Wickedness will increase and love will grow cold, but whoever endures to the end will be saved. (Matthew 24:7–10)

Man's final power on Earth before the second coming of Jesus Christ will culminate in the seven years prior to His return. For most people remaining on Earth, this will seem to be an endless nightmare, but the end will come. At this point in the revelation of this frightening period, only 1,260 days, or 3 1/2 years, remain. This is a turning point—things will get worse before the end.

Up until this point the New Roman Empire has been building up its power, conquering its enemies, and consolidating its territory. The antichrist has achieved world domination in just 3 1/2 years following the opening of the first seal. Remember just 3 1/2 years earlier?

> The Lamb breaks the first seal on the scroll, and one of the four Seraphim calls out with a voice that sounds like thunder, "Come!" A White Horse

whose rider carries a bow appears. The horseman
is crowned world leader, and he gallops away to
conquer. (Revelation 6:1–2)

Remember, the Tribulation is all about the unfinished story of
the Holy Land and the Roman Empire, and the sacrifice of Jesus
Christ. The time of the Gentiles is ending in disaster. Hallelujah!
The thousand-year reign of Jesus Christ will begin in just 3 1/2 years.

REVELATION 13:11–18. I see another strange
Animal with little horns like a lamb but with the
voice of the Dragon coming out of the Earth.
The Animal exercises the Beast's authority, and
he requires the world to worship the Beast. He
deceives the world with miracles which he is able
to perform when the Beast is present. The Animal
orders the people to make a huge statue of the
Beast and he gives breath to the statue and makes
it speak. Anyone who refuses to worship the
statue must die. Everyone on Earth is required to
get a tattoo of the name or the numerical value of
the name of the Beast on their hand or forehead.
Without the tattoo, no one can buy goods or
work. Can you interpret the name of the Beast?
His number is 666.

Suddenly, John sees another strange animal emerging—not
from the sea but from the Earth. This means it does not have power
because it is popular; its power comes from Satan and the antichrist.
It has two little horns like a lamb, but it sounds like Satan. This false
lamb is the false prophet. He is drumming up popular support for
the antichrist. This is the false lamb.

The killing of the antichrist and his coming back to life by the
indwelling of Satan is a sham of the resurrection of Jesus Christ.
The antichrist, who has been indwelt by Satan then enables the false
prophet to perform miracles. The false prophet orders the people

to make a huge statue of the antichrist, and decrees that anyone who refuses to worship the statue must die. Does he set this statue up in the temple in Jerusalem? Is this the abomination that causes desolation?

> The Desolator will make a treaty with the people for one week, but after half the week, he will stop the sacrifices and offerings. He will set up an abomination that causes desolation until the end that is decreed is poured out. (Daniel 9:27)

The Israelites suddenly know that they have been tricked, that if they refuse to worship this abomination, they will be slaughtered. They must flee (Revelation 12:6). Is Petra the place God has prepared to take care of the Israelites for 1,260 days?

Encouraged by Satan, the Antichrist blasphemes God and His temple. One of the things the antichrist has done in the first 3 1/2 years of the Tribulation is make a treaty with Israel, probably allowing them to rebuild their temple in Jerusalem. They may have just begun to worship in it. Imagine their horror when the antichrist sets up the abomination of desolation (Revelation 12:13–14) in the temple. Jesus warned us about it.

> When you see the abomination of desolation standing in the holy place, as prophesied by Daniel, then those in Judea must flee into the mountains. Those on their roofs should not even go inside to pack. (Matthew 24:15–17)

Remember, just 3 1/2 years ago?

> As the Black Horse gallops away, the Lamb breaks the fourth seal and we hear the fourth Seraphim call, "Cornel" A rider named Death approaches, riding a Pale Horse. Close behind him is another horse whose rider is named Hades. Death and

> Hades are given power to kill one-fourth of the
> Earth. They will use war, hunger, disease and
> wild animals to kill the inhabitants of the Earth.
> (Revelation 6:7–8)

The false prophet then requires everyone to receive a tattoo of the numerical value of the antichrist's name. This tattoo must be either on their forehead or their right hand, and without this tattoo, people will not be able to hold a job or purchase food. Christians are sealed by the Holy Spirit (Ephesians 1:13). The tattoo is a counterfeit seal by the false prophet. Probably a biochip will be implanted so that everyone can be tracked by computer. Now we are given a puzzle: The numerical value of the letters of the antichrist's name add up to 666. Welcome to hell on Earth.

But Satan cannot make the antichrist a god with a capital *G*. The number 6 is man's number. God's number is *7*. The number 6 is not worthy of worship. The antichrist is a false god, an idol. The false prophet is a false prophet. The New Roman Empire, the antichrist, and Satan are all interchangeable.

Today, there is an increasing trend for businesses to refuse to take money in payment for goods and services. They only want to accept credit or debit cards. This is having an impact on the poor, the homeless and the unemployed, most of whom do not use banks and cannot obtain credit. This is a foreshadowing of what will come.

Setting up a statue and forcing the people to worship it is not new. Babylonian history includes King Nebuchadnezzar, who forced his subjects to worship him.

> King Nebuchadnezzar made a golden statue 90
> feet tall which was set up on the Plain of Dura in
> Babylon. He sent messages to all of the officials of
> all the provinces of the empire to attend the dedi-
> cation… When the band plays you are to fall on
> the ground and worship King Nebuchadnezzar's
> golden statue. Anyone who refuses will be thrown
> into the flaming furnace. (Daniel 3:1–6)

The order to worship an idol is both anti-Semitic and anti-Christian, since those are the people who will refuse to worship the beast. Today, when it is easy to believe, people are not motivated. The Bible is readily available in translations that are easy to understand, but even people who go to church really haven't read the Bible. It is important to know what we believe and to believe what we know. It is important to stay in touch with God. If we do not know what we believe, we will believe lies. We will be justly judged for refusing the truth and enjoying our sins. Some two thousand years ago, Paul told us about this.

> The coming of the lawless one will be the work of Satan. With counterfeit miracles he will completely fool those who are on their way to hell because they have said "No" to the Truth. They have refused to believe the Truth and allow Him to save them. Therefore, God will allow them to believe the lie with ail their hearts, and they will be justly judged for believing falsehood, for refusing the Truth, and for enjoying their sins. (2 Thessalonians 2:9–12)

When the Tribulation arrives, the Holy Spirit is in heaven. Those who turn to the Lord will do so under the hardest of conditions. People are forced to choose God or choose Satan because judgment is imminent. Now is the time to choose not to go through the Tribulation.

> Behold, I stand at the door and knock. If anyone hears Me and opens the door, I will come in and fellowship with him and he with Me. (Revelation 3:20)

CHAPTER 14

Revelation 14:1–20

"Do nothing until God's seal can be imprinted on the foreheads of His servants." The number who will be given God's seal is 144,000. They are Children of Israel and I watch as 144,000 Israelites—12,000 from each of the 12 Tribes of Israel—receive the Seal of God on their foreheads.

—Revelation 7:3–8

REVELATION 14:1–5. The Lamb is standing on Mount Zion with the 144,000 who had received the Seal of God. They have the Name of God written on their foreheads. I hear a rushing sound and suddenly the 144,000 is a great choir singing a New Song before the Throne of God, and before the Seraphim and the 24 Elders. Only the 144,000 can sing this song because they are spiritually undefiled and blameless. They follow the Lamb wherever He goes. They are redeemed from the Earth and are a consecrated offering to God and the Lamb.

Jesus is seen on Mount Zion in heaven (Hebrews 12:22) with the 144,000 messianic Israelites who were not raptured, but who remained on Earth to witness to the children of Israel. After the Rapture, these messianic Israelites were the only Christians left on

Earth. The children of Israel are under God's protection since they fled the "abomination of desolation," so Jesus Himself gathers the 144,000 who have faithfully witnessed for Him to heaven to be with Him. There will be a crescendo of evil and judgment to the end. The final judgments are about to be poured out, and John is shown what will unfold.

Now God has sent His two witnesses to preach the Gospel to the population for 3 1/2 years.

> "I will give power to My two witnesses who are clothed in sackcloth to prophesy for 1260 days. Anyone who tries to harm these two witnesses will be consumed by fire coming from their mouths... Upon completion of the 3 1/2 years of their prophesy, the Destroyer who was freed from the bottomless pit will kill them [Revelation 9:1–11]. Their dead bodies will not be buried. They will lay exposed for 3 1/2 days in Jerusalem where Jesus Christ was crucified... But after 3 1/2 days the Holy Spirit will enter them and they will stand up. Great fear will fall on everyone, and a loud voice from Heaven will shout, "Come up!" Their enemies will watch them ascend to Heaven in a cloud. (Revelation 11:3–12)

Things are going to happen fast. Some of the events unfolding in the succeeding chapters will occur in succession but almost simultaneously. Judgment will be swift. The revelation is not repetitive—it is chronological. But events pile upon events.

> REVELATION 14:6–13. Another angel is carrying the Gospel to preach to every nation and every tribe, and in every language on Earth. The angel shouts, "Worship God the Creator and praise His greatness. The time has come when He will sit in judgment. Another angel flies

> behind him saying, "Babylon is falling because
> she seduced the nations and made them share
> in her sin." Then a third angel following them
> warns, "Anyone who worships the Antichrist and
> his statue—anyone accepting his mark must suf-
> fer the wrath of God. They will be tormented
> with fire and brimstone. The smoke of their tor-
> ture will rise forever. Encourage God's people to
> remain firm with Him to the end. Trust in Jesus."
> I hear a voice above me instructing me to write
> down, "Blessed are those who die in the Lord.
> They shall rest."

God also has an angel assigned to spread the Gospel. The end
will not come until everyone on Earth has had an opportunity to
accept or reject the salvation offered by the Lord Jesus Christ. The
wording of this passage catches our attention. I suspect that this
angel will utilize radio waves and the internet to offer the Gospel.
The message is, "Jesus Christ gave His life as the Perfect Sacrifice to
cover your sins with His blood. The time has come! Decide today
whom you will obey."

Many people believe that the destruction of Babylon revealed
here will really be upon the Babylon that existed in Iraq eons ago.
They are waiting for Babylon to be rebuilt so this scripture can be
fulfilled. That is a futile expectation. Babylon was destroyed in 478
BC by Xerxes, king of Persia, husband of Queen Esther. The city of
Babylon will never rise again because God decreed that it will never
rise again. For 2,500 years, Babylon has lain waste. Saddam Hussein
tried to rebuild it, but God said, "No!"

> Babylon, jewel of kingdoms and pride of the
> Babylonians, will be utterly destroyed by God
> like Sodom and Gomorrah. Babylon will never
> rise again. Nomads will not camp there and
> shepherds will not rest their flocks there. (Isaiah
> 13:19–20)

"Babylon" was code for Rome. The prophets could not say, "Rome will be destroyed," because they were living in the Roman Empire. They would be immediately killed for sedition and their prophecy would not be heard. However, we are given clues to the actual identity of "Babylon."

> The seven heads are seven hills on which the woman sits. (Revelation 17:9)

> All the wealth is gone in one moment. All the sea captains and crews will stand at a distance watching the smoke ascend, crying, "Woe! Woe! She made us rich. In a single hour all is gone. (Revelation 18:17–19)

We remember from our history class the myth about Romulus and Remus building Rome on seven hills. The names of those hills are Aventine, Caelian, Esquiline, Quirinal, Viminal, Capitoline, and Palatine. The merchant ships could see Rome burning from the Mediterranean Sea. You cannot See Babylon from any sea. The Tribulation will close the story of the empire that crucified Jesus Christ—the Roman Empire. Babylon is ancient history, but Rome is a principal player today.

> REVELATION 14:13–20. I see Jesus sitting on a white cloud, wearing a gold crown and holding a sharp sickle. An angel calls from the Temple, 'The time has come for you to reap. Swing the sickle." Jesus swings His sickle over the Earth, and the harvest is gathered. Another angel carrying a sickle exits the Temple, and the angel with power to destroy the Earth with fire shouts, "Use your sickle and cut off the clusters of grapes from the vines." The grapes are placed in the winepress of God's wrath, and blood flows out 200 miles.

God and Jesus and the Holy Spirit and the angels are poised for judgment. Satan, the antichrist, the false prophet, and the powers on Earth are gathering to fight to the end. Satan has read the end of the book—he knows what is coming, but he will not go down without a fight. Here we have a sneak peek at Armageddon. Blood will flow for two hundred miles. This will be human blood.

These people who die have refused to accept the salvation offered by Jesus. All that is required is to believe Him and to accept His offer. Instead, these people choose to worship the cold statue of the antichrist and accept instead his 666 mark on their foreheads.

CHAPTER 15

Revelation 15:1–8

Do not repay evil for evil. Do what is right. Do not quarrel and if possible, live in peace with everyone. Do not take revenge but leave that to God who tells us, "Vengeance is Mine; I will repay."

—Romans 12:17–19

REVELATION 15:1–4. I see another great parade in Heaven, revealing the coming events. Seven final plagues will be released on the Earth. Seven angels are assigned to deliver the seven final plagues, which will complete the Wrath of God. In addition, I see standing by a sea of fire and glass, the souls of those who have refused to bow down to the Antichrist and his statue, and who have not taken his number 666. These victorious martyrs consist of both Children of Israel as well as Christians. God has given them harps and they are singing the Song of Moses, and the Song of the Lamb. "0 Lord God Almighty, Your acts are great and marvelous. 0 King of Ages, who will not fear and glorify Your Name? All nations will worship You, for we have seen Your righteous deeds. You alone are holy."

J ohn sees a procession of the inhabitants of heaven who have been viewing the horrors occurring on Earth. All of heaven is poised for the release of the final seven plagues on the inhabitants of the Earth. Seven priestly angels who serve in the heavenly temple will deliver the wrath of God.

These are the souls of the martyrs who have refused to bow down to the evil on Earth and have refused to accept the mark of the beast. They are victorious as they stand by a sea of glass and fire—they have endured a horrible death while clinging to the Lord Jesus Christ and His promise of eternal life. They have worshiped the Good and refused to worship the evil. They have been martyred but they have not been defeated—they are victorious.

God has given harps to these victorious martyrs, and they "make a joyful noise unto the Lord" (Psalm 66:1). The Christian martyrs sing the song of the Lamb, and the Israelite martyrs sing the song of Moses. The two witnesses, probably Elijah and Enoch, and perhaps some of the messianic Israelites may be among these martyrs.

We saw the crystal clear sea before the throne of God (Revelation 4:6), but it now contains fire. It is a sea of humanity, and now the fire of persecution is evident. We do not know if there is anyone remaining on the Earth who has refused to bow down to the antichrist and receive his mark, but in view of the impending release of the wrath of God upon the Earth, it is improbable. This throng of humanity is made up of both Gentiles and Israelites. We know that the Children of Israel who are being sheltered by the Lord remain on Earth (Revelation 12:13–14), but the messianic Israelites (Revelation 7:2–8) and the two witnesses (Revelation 11:3–12) have probably been taken to heaven before the unleashing of the wrath of God upon the Earth.

God is love (1 John 4:16), but He must deal with the evil. He has not been willing that that any be lost. The Lord has stood at the door and knocked as long as possible (Matthew 7:7), but now He must move. God is angry, and He will be victorious. Satan knows this, but he will take everyone he can down with him.

> But do not forget that with the Lord a day is like
> a thousand years, and a thousand years are like a
> day. The Lord is not slow in His promised return.
> He is waiting because He is not willing that any-
> one perish. He is allowing more time for sinners
> to repent. (2 Peter 3:8–9)

John has already seen the opening of the seven seals (Revelation 6:1–8), and the sounding of the seven Trumpets (Revelation 8:1–9). These events unleashed plagues upon portions of the Earth and humanity. However, the impending pouring out of the seven bowls of the wrath of God will unleash God's fury upon the entire Earth. God's cup of wrath has reached its full measure (Genesis 15:16). Not only have the inhabitants of the Earth rejected the salvation offered by the Son of God, Jesus Christ, but they have instead turned to worship the antichrist, who is indwelled by Satan (Revelation 13:1–8).

> REVELATION 15:5–8. As I watch, the Holy of
> Holies of the Temple in Heaven is opened wide,
> and seven angels emerge from the Temple dressed
> in white linen with gold belts. These angels have
> been designated to pour out the final seven plagues
> upon the Earth. The Seraphim handed each a
> golden Bowl filled with the Wrath of God. The
> Temple is filled with smoke and no one can enter
> until the seven bowls have all been poured out.

There is a temple in heaven. The temple that Solomon built was undoubtedly modeled after the heavenly temple (1 Kings 6:1–30).

> That is why the Tabernacle on Earth was cop-
> ied from things in Heaven. All had to be made
> pure by Moses sprinkling with the blood of ani-
> mals, but the Temple in Heaven is made pure
> with a more precious offering. For Christ entered

Heaven itself and appears for us in the presence
of God. (Hebrews 9:23–24)

We see that there is a holy of holies in the heavenly temple, and
we see that it will be open when the angels prepare to pour out the
bowls of God's wrath. At the crucifixion of Jesus Christ some two
thousand years ago, the veil separating the holy of holies in the temple at Jerusalem was torn from the top to the bottom, indicating that
we now have direct access to God.

Then Jesus cried out and gave up His Spirit and
died. The curtain secluding the Holy of Holies
in the Temple was torn from top to bottom, the
Earth shook, and rocks were broken. (Matthew
27:50–51)

When Moses completed the building of the tabernacle in the
wilderness, God entered it. God was leading the children of Israel
through the wilderness in the form of a cloud.

Then the Cloud covered the Tabernacle and the
Glory of the Lord filled it. Moses was not able
to enter because the Lord filled the Tabernacle.
Whenever the Cloud lifted and moved, the peo-
ple of Israel journeyed onward, following it. But
if the Cloud stayed, they stayed until it moved.
The Cloud rested upon the Tabernacle during
the daytime, and at night there was fire in the
Cloud so that all the people of Israel could see it.
(Exodus 40:34–38)

Prior to the perfect sacrifice made by Jesus Christ, once a year
the priest would enter the holy of holies and pour blood on the
mercy seat as atonement for the sins of the people. Is the holy of
holies in heaven's temple the place where our present-day pleas for
mercy are granted? A temple will probably be built in Jerusalem at

the beginning of the Tribulation through an agreement with the antichrist (Daniel 9:27).

In heaven's temple, John sees seven angels emerge from the temple dressed in white linen with golden sashes (Exodus 28:39). They are obviously priests in the temple and are given the responsibility of pouring out the final seven bowls. These are not bowls filled with punishment to fall on portions of the Earth and its inhabitants, as was the case in the opening of the seals (Revelation 6:1–8) and the sounding of the trumpets (Revelation 8:1–9). These final bowls are filled with the wrath of God and will be poured out on the entire Earth and its inhabitants. Smoke fills heaven's temple, and no one will be able to enter and seek mercy until God's wrath is poured out upon the Earth.

This will be the final event before the return of Jesus Christ.

CHAPTER 16

Revelation 16:1–20

The Day of the Lord is coming as unexpectedly as a thief.
The heavens will disappear with a terrible roar and the
heavenly bodies will vanish in fire. The Earth and everything
on it will be burned up. Since everything around us is going
to be destroyed, we should be living holy, godly lives.

—2 Peter 3:10–11

REVELATION 16:1–12. A loud voice from the Temple commands, "Pour out the seven Bowls of the Wrath of God." The first angel pours out his Bowl over the Earth. Horrible, cancerous sores break out on everyone who has taken the mark of the Antichrist. The second angel empties his Bowl on the oceans and they look like blood. Everything in the ocean dies. The third angel declares that God is avenging the martyrdom of the saints whose blood has been spilled upon the Earth, and he pours out the contents of his Bowl upon the fresh waters which turn to blood. The fourth angel empties his Bowl upon the Sun, which causes the sun to scorch those on Earth, and they curse the Name of God. The fifth angel pours out his Bowl on the throne of the Antichrist, bringing darkness, and his subjects curse God. The sixth angel empties his Bowl on the Euphrates River, drying it up to enable the armies from the East to march unimpeded, to join in the coming battle.

Let the action begin! The Great Tribulation—the last half of the final week is ending. God's wrath is intense. The angels are poised to pour His wrath down upon the Earth. The children of Israel are protected in their hiding place. The martyrs are in heaven with the Lord. He has gathered the 144,000 witnesses to Himself, and the final two witnesses, probably Enoch and Elijah, have been martyred and have ascended to heaven. Those remaining on Earth are the hard-core who have resisted God to the end. This is their last chance to turn to God.

Some of the punishments contained in the bowls resemble some of the plagues poured out on the Egyptians when Pharaoh refused to "Let My People Go" (Exodus 7–11). Water is turned to blood (probably a massive red algae bloom), people are covered with sores, and darkness engulfs the Earth. There are even some frogs.

Everyone has cancer. Then the fourth angel pours out his bowl on the sun. God knew two thousand years ago what we were going to do to ourselves. We have been depleting ozone since the 1970s, we continue to use our manufactured refrigerants and aerosols and solvents and continue to thin the ozone layer. The Montreal Protocol, adopted in 1989, has actually begun reversing the harmful effects. Will the antichrist abide by the Montreal Protocol? It doesn't matter. Even limited nuclear war could deplete the ozone layer, and the radiation would destroy us.

There is no drinking water. There is no food. There is no light. Mankind is burning to a crisp; yet the armies receive orders to muster for battle. Do they even know what they are doing, or are they just blindly obeying Satan? Satan knows what is ahead, but he will take everyone he can just to keep them from following God. We see Satan's demons in the form of frogs. These bowls of wrath are God's final ultimatum. But Satan takes the challenge. We see Satan's demons in the form of frogs drumming up war.

REVELATION 16:13–18. Three evil spirits, which look like frogs, leap from the mouths of Satan, the Antichrist, and his False Prophet. These demons gathered all of the rulers of the Earth to fight against the Lamb of God on the Day of Judgment. The Lamb says "I will come as unexpectedly as a thief. Blessed are those who keep themselves ready." The armies are gathering north of Jerusalem on the Plain of Megiddo to fight the Battle of Armageddon. As the seventh angel pours the final Bowl of Wrath into the air, I hear a shout from the Throne of God declaring, "It is finished!" Thunder roars and lightning crashes, and the greatest earthquake ever felt shakes the Earth.

When Jesus Christ was dying on the cross two thousand years ago, He completed God's plan for our salvation. He was the ultimate sacrifice, and His blood covers our sins perfectly. He was, "obedient even to death on the Cross" (Philippians 2:8). His final words on the cross were, "It is finished" (John 19:28–30). Now, God's plan for judgment is completed. Now, we hear God the Father sitting on His throne in heaven say, "It is finished!"

The sound of His voice causes the Earth to shutter. There is a great storm followed by the greatest earthquake ever to shake this world. God's punctuation is also perfect.

REVELATION 16:19–20. Cities all over the Earth fall in heaps of rubble. Babylon is split into three sections, and she is punished with the last drop of wine in God's Bowl of Wrath. Mountains are flattened, and the islands disappear. Hundred-pound hailstones fall upon the Earth, crushing people, but the people continue to curse God.

The seat of the antichrist is split into three sections. Remember the saga: Rome was built by Romulus and Remus on seven hills beside the Tiber River? There is not strong seismic activity in Rome, but there is tectonic activity in the mountains to the east of Rome. Some 1,500 years ago an earthquake destroyed the Colosseum. Scientists think a north-south fault system in the Apennine chain of mountains northeast of Rome caused that destruction. Also, Mount Vesuvius, a very active volcano, sits on an east-west fault line located some 140 miles south of Rome near Naples. Rome, not Babylon, is destined to be split into three sections by the greatest earthquake in history.

To add insult to injury, the Earth will be pounded by hundred-pound hailstones. Scientists estimate that a hailstone of that weight would be about 30 inches in diameter—more than two feet across! Deadly to anything alive and pulverizing to the damaged buildings. You would not be safe in an army tank!

And then she will burn!

CHAPTER 17

Revelation 17:1–18

Babylon, like Sodom and Gomorrah, will be overthrown by God. She will never be inhabited again through all generations.

—Isaiah 13:20

REVELATION 17:1–5. One of the seven angels who poured out the wrath of God says, "Come and I'll show you the punishment of the great prostitute. The world's rulers have had immoral relations with her, and the populations have been drunk on the wine of her immorality." In the desert I see a woman wearing purple and scarlet clothes and beautiful jewelry, who is sitting upon a scarlet beast with seven heads and 10 horns. The woman holds a golden goblet filled with obscenities. On her forehead is written "Babylon the Great, Mother of Prostitutes and Idol Worship in the world."

The angel shows John a glimpse of the far distant future. He calls the woman "Babylon," but she is, in fact, Rome. We remember the ancient myth about Romulus and Remus and the founding of Rome on seven hills in 753 BC. The prostitute pictured here cannot be Babylon, because that city was destroyed in 478 BC. Isaiah prophesied that Babylon would never be inhabited again, and that prophecy has been fulfilled to this day. Not even Saddam Hussein could bring Babylon back.

> The whole world spoke one language. They moved eastward to the Plain of Shinar and settled there. They made bricks and baked them. Using tar as mortar, they built a city, so that they would not be scattered abroad. "Let us build a tower which reaches Heaven and make a name for ourselves." But the Lord said, "If they speak the same language nothing will be impossible for them. We will confuse their language." So the Lord scattered them over the whole Earth. It was called Babel because there the Lord confused the language and scattered them over the Earth.—(Genesis 11:1–9)

Babylon was one of the earliest cities and was a seat of power of Noah's grandson, Nimrod (Genesis 10:8–12). That was probably around 1700 BC. Then some 1,100 years later, Babylon was the seat of power of King Nebuchadnezzar when the children of Israel were carried into captivity for 70 years. Babylon was the first of the empires revealed to Nebuchadnezzar and the prophet Daniel (Daniel 7:2–8). Around 700 BC, the prophet Isaiah had foretold that God would destroy Babylon and that it would never be inhabited again (Isaiah 13). Babylon was destroyed in 478 BC by Queen Esther's husband, King Xerxes (Ahasuerus). It has never again been inhabited.

God showed the prophet Daniel the empires that would exist until the end of the world as we know it: Babylon, Persia, Greece, Rome, and the New Roman Empire, which would be ruled by the antichrist and Satan (Daniel 7:2–8). Daniel described Rome and the New Roman Empire, which grew out of it.

> After that I saw a fourth beast [Rome]. It had large iron teeth. It trampled and devoured its victims. It had 10 horns and was different from the

> other beasts. While I thought about the horns,
> another little horn [New Roman Empire] came
> up among them, uprooting three of the first
> horns. This horn had the eyes of a man and a
> boastful mouth. (Daniel 7:2–8)

We remember that the apostle John tells us that he has also seen this beast.

> I see a strange Creature [Antichrist] which had
> seven heads and 10 horns wearing crowns arising
> up out of the sea. Blasphemous names insulting
> God were written on each head. It looked like a
> leopard, with a lion's mouth and a bear's feet. The
> Dragon [Satan] gives the Creature his own power
> and authority and crown. One of the heads has a
> fatal wound, but the wound is healed. The peo-
> ple are in awe and worship the Creature and the
> Dragon for giving him such power. "Who is able
> to fight against him?" (Revelation 13:1–4)

The Roman Empire was never conquered; it just fell apart. In AD 330, acting to reunify the Roman Empire and for better defense, the emperor Constantine moved the throne from Rome to Constantinople. Today, Constantinople is the city Istanbul, Turkey. Leadership of Rome was left in the hands of the church.

Following World War II, in a movement for economic and polit-ical peace, an effort began to unite European countries. The six found-ing countries were Belgium, France, Germany, Italy, Luxembourg, and the Netherlands. In 1957, the European Economic Community (the common market) was established. Denmark, Ireland, and the United Kingdom joined the European Community in 1973. Then, on November 1, 1993, the European Union was founded. It was headquartered in Brussels, Belgium, with twenty-seven members. The Roman Empire had morphed into the European Union.

The European Union adopted stamps and coins portraying the ancient Greek goddess Europa riding on a bull—the Greek god Zeus. We see this picture here in Revelation 17:1–5. They adopted a flag showing twelve gold stars arranged in a circle of unity on a blue background. The European Union parliament building is located in Strasbourg, France, and is modeled after the ancient Tower of Babel. Is this one reason the New Roman Empire is called "Babylon" in the Revelation?

> REVELATION 17:6–18. I can see the prostitute is drunk on the blood of the martyrs. The angel asks me, "Why are you surprised? I can tell you who she is. The animal she rides was alive but is now dead. Soon he will come out of the bottomless pit and go to perdition. The people on Earth whose names are not written in the Lamb's Book of Life will be surprised at his appearance, since he is dead. The seven heads are seven hills on which she sits. Also, they are seven rulers: Five have fallen, and one now rules. Then one will come for a short time. The Beast is an eighth ruler going to his destruction. The creature's 10 horns represent 10 kings who will sign a treaty giving the Beast power, and together they will battle against the Lamb. The Lamb will conquer them. He is the King of kings and His followers are faithful. The waters where the prostitute sits are multitudes of people. The Beast and the kings will hate her and will bring her down and burn her with fire. The woman is the city which rules the world.

Notice that the Roman Empire had ten heads, and the New Roman Empire has seven heads. Is Brexit showing us the uprooting of the first of the three uprooted heads?

The leaders of the European countries will give their authority to the antichrist and fulfill God's plan. The multitudes of people on the Earth are shown as waters upon which the woman sits. The antichrist will be a very popular leader. Remember, he will come in riding a white horse (Revelation 6:1–2).

Will the antichrist set up his headquarters in Rome? Will he be a Roman? Why will the horns, or kings, all hate the woman—Rome? Why will they will attack and burn her?

CHAPTER 18

Revelation 18:1–24

Cities all over the Earth fall in heaps of rubble. Babylon is split into three sections, and she is punished with the last drop of wine in God's Bowl of Wrath.

—Revelation 16:19

REVELATION 18:1–8. I see an angel with great authority coming down from Heaven, and the Earth was brightened by his splendor. He shouts, "Babylon is fallen. She has become a den of every kind of evil spirit. Kings and Nations have drunk of her immorality and businessmen have become rich from her excesses." I heard another voice from Heaven call out, "Come away. Do not participate in her sins or you will be punished with her. Her sins are piled up to Heaven and God is ready to judge her for her crimes. She brewed woe for others; give her a double portion from her own cup. She boasts, 'I am queen and I will never mourn.' Therefore, death and mourning and famine will overtake her in one day, and she shall be consumed by fire. Mighty is the Lord God who judges her."

The angel's proclamation is fulfilled.

> Another angel flies behind him saying, "Babylon is falling because she seduced the nations and made them share in her sin." (Revelation 14:8)

At the time Babylon conquered Judah and carried God's people away into slavery, the prophet Jeremiah warned the people not to get comfortable there—Babylon would be destroyed.

> Run! Flee from Babylon! Do not be destroyed with her. The time for God's vengeance has come. She has made the whole world drunk from the wine in her cup, and they have gone mad. (Jeremiah 51:6–7)

Here, probably some 2,600 years later, we again hear a voice from Heaven calling on the people to, "Come away! Do not participate in her sins."

During the Tribulation, the population of the world has been dramatically reduced because of constant warfare, pollution, global warming, hunger, and wild animals. Satan has been thrown out of heaven and down on Earth, he has indwelled the antichrist (Revelation 12:7–12). The Holy Spirit has withdrawn to heaven, the 144,000 messianic Israelites have been taken to heaven (Revelation 14:1–5), and there has been wholesale martyrdom of the Christians and their souls are in heaven (Revelation 7:9–17). God is sheltering the Israelites in a place prepared for them (Revelation 12:15–17).

Likely, the remaining sordid society of Rome has reverted to ancient Roman ways, such as daily battles between slaves and lions in the modern-day Colosseum—the Stadio Olimpico. The people are either very rich or very poor; the middle class has succumbed. Inflation is rampant and starvation is rampant.

The antichrist and Satan have made Rome their headquarters, even though the headquarters of the European Union probably remains in Brussels, Belgium. The false prophet is settled in at the

Vatican. They control the nations—they do not need those people in Brussels. But the unholy trinity isn't at home. They have already set out for Armageddon (Revelation 16:16).

> REVELATION 18:9-20. When the rulers who shared in her immorality see the smoke rising from her, they will be terrified, and will stand afar crying, "Woe, woe! In one day your doom is come!" The merchants of Earth will stand away weeping, for there is no one left to buy their gold and silver, precious stones, pearls, fine linen and silks, woods and carvings, ivory, brass, iron and marble, spices, perfumes, ointments, wine, olive oil, fine flour, animals and chariots and slaves. All the fine things you prized will never be yours again. "Woe, woe! That beautiful city, dressed in purple and scarlet and fine jewelry! All the wealth gone in one moment." The sea captains and crews will stand at a distance as the smoke ascends, crying, "Woe, woe! Great city. She made us rich. In a single hour all is gone."

Rome has been an important city for some 2,600 years. It was the capital city of the Roman Empire, so it was the capital city of the world at the time of Jesus Christ. Rome was a pagan empire, and the Romans presided over the crucifixion of Jesus Christ circa AD 33 (John 19:21–30). Then some 37 years later, Jerusalem was leveled by the Romans under the leadership of the Roman general Titus, son of the Roman Emperor Vespasian.

Christianity was an underground religion in Rome. Jews and Christians buried their dead in the underground Catacombs, and they are an important repository of early Christian art. While Paul was preaching the Gospel in Greece around AD 56, Rome was already calling him. He got a head start on his planned missionary journey to Rome by writing the epistle to the Romans. However, his journey to Rome didn't go as planned. God was in control. Paul went to Rome as a prisoner instead.

Upon Paul's return to Jerusalem, he was arrested, accused of sneaking Gentiles into the temple (Acts 21:27–37). While under arrest in Caesarea, as a prisoner Paul was able to witness to (1) the Roman commander, to (2) Felix, the Roman governor of Judea, to (3) Festus, the succeeding governor of Judea, to (4) King Herod Agrippa (Acts 24–26), and finally to (5) Nero. He appealed his case to the emperor in Rome (Acts 27). While in Rome, Paul was not in prison but lived in a house under guard, where he was allowed to freely preach the Gospel (Acts 28:14–31).

Luke did not write a sequel to the Acts of the Apostles, but it is believed Paul appeared before the Emperor Nero around AD 63 and was acquitted. (The burning of Rome while Nero fiddled occurred in AD 64.) Tradition holds that Paul was arrested again and was beheaded in Rome—probably around the end of Nero's reign in AD 67, and that the apostle Peter was crucified in Rome around the same time.

Peter's wife accompanied him to Rome, and in his first letter, he wrote that she and Mark were with him.

> She is in Babylon and sends greetings, as does
> Mark. (1 Peter 5:13)

"Babylon" was a code name for Rome. Christians could not say bad things about Rome. That would have gotten them thrown to the lions. Some 250 years later, a basilica was built over Peter's grave, and that was the beginning of the Vatican. In AD 313, the emperor Constantine embraced Christianity.

> With the Trumpet call of God and with a loud
> command, the dead will rise first. Then, we who
> are still alive will be caught up with them in the
> clouds and we will be with the Lord forever. (1
> Thessalonians 4:16–17)

Following the Rapture of Christians, described by Paul in 1 Thessalonians, the false prophet will probably take up residence in the vacated Vatican. We get a glimpse of this with the flying of the yellow flag in battle led by the unholy trinity. The Vatican flag is the only yellow flag.

> When the demons are freed, they muster an army of 200 million warriors empowered to kill a third of all the people on Earth. Most of the warriors are wearing red breastplates, but some wear sky blue and yellow breastplates. (Revelation 9:17)

Like Sodom and Gomorrah, apparently Rome will be destroyed in one day.

> Then God rained burning sulfur down from Heaven on Sodom and Gomorrah. The Lord destroyed the cities and the people living in them, as well as the entire plain and the vegetation. (Genesis 19:24–25)

God destroyed Sodom and Gomorrah some four thousand years ago. Like those cities, Rome will be destroyed in one day. The antichrist will not be fiddling while Rome burns this time. Satan, the false prophet, and the antichrist will be moving toward the Plain of Megiddo to fight the Battle of Armageddon.

> REVELATION 18:21–24. O Heaven, O Children of God, O Prophets and Apostles, rejoice over her fate! At last God has given you judgment against her. A mighty angel picked up a boulder like a millstone and threw it into the sea. "That great city Babylon shall be thrown down and she will disappear forever. Never again will the sound of music be heard, no harps or trumpets. No trade will ever again exist there. Never

again will the light of a lamp shine in a window,
or the voices of a bride and groom be heard. She
has deceived the world with her sorcery; she has
shed the blood of the martyred saints."

Like Babylon and like Sodom and Gomorrah, Rome is gone
forever. As an exclamation point, an angel throws a meteor into the
Mediterranean Sea. Will that cause a tidal wave to extinguish the fire?

Babylon, jewel of kingdoms, will be overthrown
by God. Like Sodom and Gomorrah, she will
never be inhabited again. (Isaiah 13:17–20)

CHAPTER 19

Revelation 19:1–21

Blow the trumpet and sound the alarm in Zion. Let everyone tremble, for the Day of the Lord is coming. It is a day of clouds and darkness and doom. A mighty army spreading like dawn across the mountains; never before and never again such an army.

—Joel 2:1–2

REVELATION 19:1–10. A huge crowd in Heaven is shouting, "Hallelujah! God has punished the Great Prostitute and He has avenged the murder of His servants. Praise the Lord!" The Elders and the Seraphim worshiped God, "Amen. Praise the Lord!" I hear what sounds like the waves of a hundred oceans. It is the sound of a huge crowd shouting, "Praise the Lord! The time has come for the Wedding Banquet of the Lamb. His Bride is wearing the cleanest, whitest, finest linen. She is dressed in the good deeds performed by God's people." The angel who is with me says, "God has blessed those who are invited to the Wedding Banquet of the Lamb." I fall at the feet of the angel, and he admonishes me, "Don't. I am a servant of God, just as you and all Christians are. The purpose of the prophecy which I have shown you is to tell about Jesus."

J ewish wedding traditions are clearly seen in the Gospels. When the decision was made to marry, the couple would prepare by cleansing by immersion in water—mikvah. We see this as baptism, and Jesus took care of this when He was baptized by John the Baptist (Matthew 3:13–17). Then they enter a binding marriage contract—huppah. The couple is married, but the marriage is not consummated. Today, Christians are in this stage of the marriage. This is a binding contract; to break the contract the husband must obtain a divorce—a get.

The groom prepares a place for the couple to live, and the bride prepares for the wedding and her move into the new home—erusin. Jesus is in heaven preparing a place for us (John 14:2–3), and we are preparing our fine white linen wedding garments. We are anxiously waiting for our Groom to carry us to the place He has prepared for us—nissuin. He will carry us home with much fanfare (1 Thessalonians 4:15–17). At the Rapture, we will consummate the marriage and spend seven years in seclusion. Then there will be a great marriage feast. Will grace, or Birkat Hamazon, be followed by the pouring of two glasses of wine into a third glass, symbolizing the creation of a new life together—Sheva Brachot?

On His way to the Battle of Armageddon, Jesus and His bride will stop by for the wife of God. Where has God been sheltering her for the final half of the Tribulation? For 2,700 years, we have had a glimpse of this moment. Isaiah told us that Jesus would come from Edom (Jordan). That strengthens the thought that God will shelter the children of Israel in the ancient city of Petra through the last half of the Tribulation.

> Who is coming from Edom wearing splendid blood-stained garments? Who is marching forward with great strength? "It is I, able to save." Why are your garments stained with blood? "I have trod the winepress alone. No Nation was with Me." (Isaiah 63:1–3)

This meeting of Jesus Christ and the wife of God will bring fulfillment of the Day of Atonement, established by God in the Sinai desert way back some 3,400 years ago. Isn't God's plan remarkable?

> The Lord said to Moses, "The 10th day of the seventh month is the Day of Atonement. Deny yourselves and assemble to present a burnt offering. Do not work on that day. Make atonement for yourselves before the Lord. (Leviticus 23:26–28)

Zechariah told us that the meeting of Jesus and the children of Israel will be quite emotional. He told us how sad and how joyful it will be. But by His grace they will be victorious. They will see the Light of the World and will recognize Him as the Son of God, and they will spend eternity with Him.

> I will pour out on the House of David a spirit of grace. They will see Me whom they have pierced, and they will mourn for Him as for an only child. They will grieve bitterly as for a firstborn son. (Zechariah 12:10)

> Then the Lord will fight against the Nations. On that day He will stand on the Mount of Olives east of Jerusalem, and it will split from east to west, with half of the mountain moving north and half moving south. Living water will flow from Jerusalem to the Dead Sea and to the Mediterranean Sea. The Lord will be King over the whole Earth. (Zechariah 14:3–8)

> REVELATION 19:11–16. Heaven opens, and I see one called Faithful and True sitting on a White horse. His eyes are like flames and there are many crowns on His head. Only He knows

the meaning of the Name written on His forehead. His clothes are dipped in blood, for He has
trod the winepress of the wrath of God Almighty.
He is The Word of God, and in His mouth is a
sharp sword to subdue the Nations. The armies
of Heaven follow Him, dressed in white and
mounted on white horses. He will rule with an
iron fist. On His robe is written "King of kings,
and Lord of lords."

Paul also told us about the second coming of Jesus Christ.

God is just, and He will avenge your suffering
when the Lord Jesus is revealed descending from
Heaven in blazing fire with His angels. He will
punish those who do not accept the Gospel with
everlasting destruction and exclusion from the
presence of the Lord. (2 Thessalonians 1:6–9)

The millennial reign of Jesus Christ will fulfill the seventh of
the feasts of the Lord set out in Leviticus—the Feast of Tabernacles,
or Booths—Sukkot. He will "tabernacle" with us for a thousand
years. The people will camp on the streets of, and on the hillsides surrounding Jerusalem. The Feast of Tabernacles occurs in September or
October of each year. In 2020. This feast will begin on the evening of
October 2 and will end on the evening of October 9.

The Lord instructed Moses, "Tell the Israelites
that on the 15th day of the seventh month the
Feast of Tabernacles begins. Do not work on the
first day, but hold a sacred assembly and present
a burnt offering. You will present burnt offerings
for seven days. Do no work on the eighth day,
but hold a closing sacred assembly and present a
burnt offering. (Leviticus 23:33–36)

Jesus Christ has work to do. The Word, His bride dressed in fine white linen, and the army of heaven move westward "like dawn across the mountains" (Joel 2:2) to face the unholy trinity and their army at the Battle of Armageddon. He is the Word of God. Just as when He created the universe, all He has to do is speak and *bang!* It is done.

> In the Beginning God created the Heavens and the Earth. The Earth was dark and empty. God's Holy Spirit hovered over the waters, and the Word of God said, "Let there be Light," and there was Light. (Genesis 1:1–3)
>
> In the Beginning was the Word. The Word was with God. The Word was God. From the beginning He was with God. By His Word, God created everything. In His Word was life, and that life was the Light of Men. The Light shines in the darkness, but the darkness has not understood. (John 1:1–5)

The darkness is about to hear the Word of God. It is all over before it even begins.

> REVELATION 19:17–21. I see an angel standing in the sunshine calling to the birds, "Come and eat the flesh of humanity, both great and small." The Antichrist and the False Prophet are gathering the Earth's armies against the armies of Christ. Both the Antichrist and the False Prophet are thrown into the Lake of Fire. Christ kills their entire army with the sharp sword of His Word. All the birds of the heavens are gorged with their flesh.

This takes us back to the beginning of our Bible. Satan appeared to Eve in the form of a serpent in the garden of Eden and enticed her to disobey God. At that time, God told Satan that he would strike His heel, which is our first glimpse of the death of Christ on the cross. But the Word of God, Jesus Christ, will destroy Satan.

> God Said to the serpent, "You are cursed above all creatures. You and her Offspring will be enemies. You will strike His heel, but He will crush your head. (Genesis 3:14–15)

The Word will rule in peace on Earth for a thousand years.

> The Lord says, "I love Zion. I will return to Zion, My Holy Mountain. I will dwell in Jerusalem which will be called the City of Truth. Old men and women with walking canes will sit in the streets where children are playing." (Zechariah 8:2–5)

Upon His second coming, Jesus will establish His millennial kingdom. In one day, He will remove the iniquity of the land. Then there will be a thousand years of peace. The peace which God gives us today is peace between us and Him. In the millennium, there will also be peace between us and our neighbors.

> The wolf and the lamb will live together; the leopard will lie down with the goat and the lion and the calf, and a little child will lead them. (Isaiah 11:6)

CHAPTER 20

Revelation 20:1–15

In the last days, the Temple Mount will be raised above the hills and people will say, "Let us go up to the Lord's mountain. He will teach us so that we may walk in His ways.

—Micah 4:1–2

REVELATION 20:1–3. Another angel is coming from Heaven. He holds a heavy chain and the key to the bottomless pit. He binds up the Dragon, Satan, in chains and he locks Satan in the bottomless pit for 1000 years. Satan will not be able to mislead the nations until the 1000 years are finished, and then he will be released for a little while.

The antichrist and the false prophet have been thrown into the Lake of Fire (Revelation 19:20). Now, Satan is thrown into the bottomless pit. The unholy trinity will not be able to make trouble or mislead people for the next one thousand years—the millennial reign of Jesus Christ will be peaceful.

The Lord showed the prophet Ezekiel a vision of the millennial temple (Ezekiel 40–48). Sacrifices will be made on holy days. Why will sacrifices be made more than two thousand years after Jesus Christ gave His life as the perfect sacrifice and His blood covers our sins?

> There was a room by each of the inner gateways
> where burnt offerings were washed. There were
> two tables on each side where the burnt, sin,
> and guilt offerings were slaughtered. (Ezekiel
> 40:38–39)

The Lord keeps very accurate records. Along the way, the children of Israel began to worship idols and began to look with disdain at their offerings to the Lord. The Lord rejected their offerings. The sacrifices that they made were unacceptable to God.

> A son honors his father. Where is the respect due
> Me? O priests, you show contempt for My name
> by placing defiled food on My Altar. You ask,
> "How have we disrespected You?" You say the
> Lord's table is contemptible, but you bring blind,
> crippled, and diseased animals. That is wrong!
> Offer them to your governor. Would he accept
> this? (Malachi 1:6–8)

The temple where they made sacrifices was destroyed in AD 70, and they were scattered until May 14, 1945. The temple has not yet been rebuilt. They owe God a huge number of sacrifices. This is a debt owed to God.

Remember, the Lord also required that the land lie fallow every seventh year. They, likewise, had not been obeying this command.

> The Lord told Moses, "The land must observe a
> sabbath to the Lord. Sow your fields for six years,
> but in the seventh year do not sow your fields
> or prune your vineyards. The land is to have a
> year of rest. Whatever the land produces may be
> eaten." (Leviticus 25:1–7)

The Lord exacted this rest which was owed to the land during the seventy years the Jews were in exile in Babylon.

> Nebuchadnezzar carried the remnant into exile
> in Babylon. The land enjoyed its sabbath rests.
> It rested until the 70 years were completed in
> fulfillment of the Word of the Lord spoken by
> Jeremiah. (2 Chronicles 36:20–21)

God keeps good records. He knows precisely how many sacrifices the Israelites owe Him. During the millennial reign, they will willingly fellowship with Him, and He will exact the sacrifices that are owed to Him. These sacrifices will not be memorials to the death of Jesus Christ, our perfect Sacrifice. They will be atonement for their failure to give the Lord His holidays. The Feasts of the Lord were just that. He brought the people together to fellowship with Him and with each other. They were to have a big barbecue three times a year. They will do that during Christ's millennial reign.

The preincarnate Jesus Christ gave the prophet Ezekiel a tour of the millennial temple some 2,500 years ago (Ezekiel 40–48). On the south side of a high mountain were buildings, which looked like a city. Jesus was measuring everything with a measuring cord. There was a wall surrounding the temple area, which had gates at the east, west, north, and south. There will be rooms for the priests and for the preparation of the sacrifices. The Levites will prepare the sacrifices.

The temple will sit on a portion of the land belonging to the Lord. The land to the north and south of that holy land will be divided among the tribes of Jacob. The name of the city will be "The Lord is there."

> REVELATION 20:4–6. I see thrones, set up
> for those who are given the right to judge. The
> souls of those martyred for testifying for Jesus,
> who had not worshiped the Antichrist or his
> statue, nor received his mark, will reign with
> Christ for 1,000 years. These are believers who
> have died during the Tribulation. This is the First
> Resurrection. The remainder of the dead will not
> come back to life until the end of the Millennial

Reign. Those who share in the First Resurrection
are blessed. They will not experience the Second
Death. They will be priests to God and Christ.

These are people who are not believers prior to the Rapture, but
they turn to Christ during the Tribulation, and many are killed for
their belief. They will not have the indwelling of the Holy Spirit, so it
will be harder, but they will be firm in their belief. They will refuse to
worship the antichrist or his statue, and they will not take the mark
of the beast (Revelation 13:11–17). We first see some of their souls
waiting under the altar in heaven during the Tribulation (Revelation
5:9–11).

This group probably does not include any of the 144,000 messianic Jews who are believers, but who also will not be Raptured. They
will remain on Earth to witness to God's wife during the Tribulation.
The 144,000 will receive the protective seal of the Living God
(Revelation 7:1–8). Apparently, none are martyred, because we later
see them with the Lamb in heaven (Revelation 14:1–5).

These souls will be judged for their good deeds.

I have set up a Book of Remembrance for those
who fear and worship Me. They are my treasured
jewels, and I will spare them, just as a man spares
his own son who serves him. (Malachi 20:11–12)

REVELATION 20:7–10. When the 1000 years
is completed, Satan is released from the bottomless pit to recruit Gog and Magog to battle against
God's people outside of Jerusalem, but the armies
are consumed by fire from God. Satan is thrown
into the Lake of Fire where the Antichrist and
the False Prophet have been since Armageddon.
They will be tormented forever.

Prophesy against Gog, and the Land of Magog,
chief prince of Mesheck and Tubal. I will defeat

you and those making war. Persia, Cush, Put, Gomer and Togarmah will be with them. (Ezekiel 38:1–6)

These named are descendants of Noah. After the flood, his sons were dispersed throughout Europe, Africa, and the Middle East. (Genesis 10).

Gog was apparently a later descendant of Noah's son, Japheth.

Magog, Meshech, and Tubal were Noah's grandsons and Japheth's sons. They settled in Turkey.

Gomer was Noah's grandson and Japheth's son. He settled in Russia.

Togarmah was Noah's great-grandson, grandson of Japheth, and son of Gomer. He settled in Turkey.

Cush was Noah's grandson and Ham's son. He settled in Egypt.

Put was Noah's grandson and Ham's son. He settled in Libya.

Persia (Iran) was a latecomer. Persia did not come on the scene until God empowered this land of Nomads to defeat the Babylonian Empire in one night and end the Babylonian captivity of the Jews. (God's people were first called "Jews" in Babylon.) Perhaps the Persians were descendants of Japheth's son Madai, who moved south of the Caspian Sea in the area of Tehran. Persia's first king, Cyrus II or Cyrus the Great, lived 601–530 BC. In 539 BC, the first year of his reign, Cyrus commissioned the Jews to return to Jerusalem and rebuild the temple (Ezra 1:1–2).

People have been living in peace for a thousand years because Satan has been locked away, but Satan and a lot of humans have not learned the lesson. They have not learned to love peace. As soon as Satan is released from the bottomless pit at the end of the millennial reign of Christ, they want to start a war.

But they are consumed by fire, and Satan is thrown into the Lake of Fire. The unholy trinity, Satan, the antichrist, and the false prophet have met their end.

REVELATION 20:11–15. I see a great White Throne. The Earth and sky flee from the face of

God. The dead are standing before God, and the Books, including the Book of Life, are opened. Those buried in the oceans, and in the earth give up their dead, who will receive judgment based upon their deeds written down in the Books. Death and Hades are thrown into the Lake of Fire. This is the Second Death, and anyone whose name is not recorded in the Book of Life is thrown into the Lake of Fire.

This is the final judgment. On trial are those who refused to turn to God. God keeps very good records. He has it all written down to be used as evidence either for or against those on trial. They will be judged on God's records of their deeds.

The prophet Daniel also had a vision of the judgment following the Tribulation.

As I looked, thrones appeared. The Ancient of Days in white clothing, with hair as white as wool, sat on His flaming throne. The wheels of the throne were blazing and a river of fire was flowing before Him. He was attended by thousands, and millions stood before Him. When the court was seated, the books were opened. (Daniel 7:9–10)

CHAPTER 21

Revelation 21:1–27

Violence and destruction will not be heard in your land,
You will call your walls Salvation and Praise will be your gates.
No longer will the sun be your light, nor
will the moon shine on you.
The Lord will be your Everlasting Light; God will be your Glory.

—Isaiah 60:18–19

REVELATION 21:1–8. The Earth and sky have disappeared, but I see a new sky and a new Earth with no oceans. Then I see the New Jerusalem descending from Heaven. It is a glorious sight. Listen to the shout coming from the Throne, "God will dwell among men. They will be His people and He will be their God. There will be no more death nor sorrow nor pain." The Lord announces, "I Am making all things new. I Am the A and the Z, the Beginning and the End. I will give the Water of Life to everyone who is thirsty. Everyone who conquers will inherit these blessings, but cowards who are unfaithful to Me, murderers, and the corrupt, and the immoral are doomed to the Lake of Fire."

R emember, the Earth and sky that we know fled before the judgment seat.

> I see a great White Throne. The Earth and sky
> flee from the face of God. (Revelation 20:11)

Talk about heaven on Earth! The final judgment has been carried out. The only people remaining are those whose names are written in the Book of Life. Only God's people remain. But where are they? Suspended in space? The whole universe has felt another bang!

Satan and those who rejected the Lord and His ways are forever in the lake of fire—the place prepared for them. Things have been rearranged. God has prepared a new place for us also. The New Jerusalem and the New Earth will be the everlasting home of God and Jesus, and the home of those whose names are written in the Book of Life. Are we the capitol of the universe?

> You have come to the heavenly Jerusalem, the
> city of the Living God, to thousands of joyful
> angels, to the Church whose names are written in
> Heaven and to the spirits of righteous men made
> perfect, to God the Judge, to Jesus the Mediator,
> and to the sprinkled Blood. (Hebrews 12:22–24)

There are no oceans on the New Earth. The Earth that we know is 71 percent oceans, and they separate the countries and the peoples. Who will inhabit the New Earth? Will it be inhabited by the children of Israel? By the nationals? Will the land be allocated? We understand that there will be God the Father, God the Son, angels and seraphim and cherubim, and Christians living in the New Jerusalem. Will people with glorified bodies need food? We know that after Jesus Christ was resurrected, He ate. Can you grow food in streets of gold? Will the tree of life be the only growing vegetation in the New Jerusalem? Will the New Earth be cultivated?

He showed them His hands and feet, but they were in disbelief and amazement and joy. He asked them, "Do you have any food? They gave him a piece of fish and He ate it. (Luke 24:40–43)

Will there be rivers and lakes of fresh water, and will there be fish?

REVELATION 21:9–21. One of the seven angels who had poured out his flask of the wrath of God comes to me. "I will show you the Bride. He takes me to a mountain peak and I watch the New Jerusalem, home of the Bride, as it descends from the skies. It appears to be a clear crystal cube filled with the Glory of God. The angel measures the city with a gold rod. The sides of the cube measure 1500 miles in length, in width, and in height. The walls made of jasper are 216 feet thick, with 12 gates, each made of a single pearl. There are three gates on each of the eastern, northern, southern and western sides of the City. The names of the 12 Tribes of Israel are written on the gates. The names of the 12 Apostles are written on the 12 foundation stones made of jasper, sapphire, chalcedony, emerald, sardonyx, carnelian, chrysolite, beryl, topaz, chrysoprase, turquoise, and amethyst. The city is made of pure gold, as transparent as glass.

The stones of the foundation of the New Jerusalem are the same as the stones that decorated the breastplates of the priests (Exodus 39:10–13). However, the names of the apostles rather than the names of the tribes of Israel will be written on the foundation stones of the New Jerusalem

The New Jerusalem is descending from heaven. Will it remain suspended above the Earth like a satellite? Or will it come to rest on the New Earth? A cube 1,500 miles tall and 1,500 miles across could cause the Earth to wobble on its axis, so the New Jerusalem may be suspended above the Earth. The people in their glorified bodies will be able to transport themselves, as Jesus did after His resurrection (Matthew 28:8–10).

> REVELATION 21:22–27. There is not a Temple in the City, and the Sun and the Moon are not visible, because God and the Lamb are the Light. Since there is no night, the gates will never close. The honor of the Nations will be brought in. Nothing impure will be permitted. Only those whose names are written in the Book of Life will enter.

We are not told that the children of Israel, the wife of God, will live in the New Jerusalem. They were always promised the land. Probably they will be given land on the New Earth. It will be pristine, and the gates of the New Jerusalem will never close, so they could come and go. And God will probably visit with them. We know that God visited with Adam and Eve on Earth prior to their disobedience.

> Then Adam and Eve heard the sound of the Lord as He was walking in the garden in the cool of the day. They hid in the trees, but the Lord called, "Where are you?" (Genesis 3:8–9)

We are told that the "honor of the Nations" will be brought in. We know that there were people in Old Testament times who were not Israelites. They were from other nations, but they knew God. Cyrus the Great immediately comes to mind. When this Persian king conquered Babylon, he immediately allowed the Jewish captives to return to Jerusalem to rebuild the temple. He said, "The Lord God of Heaven has given me the kingdoms of the Earth, and He has appointed me to build a Temple for Him at Jerusalem" (Ezra 1:2). A hundred years earlier, the prophet Isaiah had said, "The Lord says to

Cyrus, His anointed, 'I take hold of his right hand to subdue Nations before him'" (Isaiah 45:1).

We remember that there were many Old Testament heroes and heroines who were not Israelites, but who knew God. There were probably thousands and thousands not mentioned in the Bible. It seems that they will also reside on the New Earth. We can name a few.

There was Naaman, the Syrian, who came to Elisha for healing of his leprosy. He said, "Now I know there is no god in all the world except the God of Israel" (2 Kings 5:15).

Rahab of Jericho knew that God was leading the children of Israel on their return from Egypt. She hid and protected the Israelite spies who were reconnoitering in advance of their reentry into the promised land. She said, "For the Lord your God is God in Heaven and on Earth (Joshua 2:11).

Then there was Obed-Edom, the Gittite, or Philistine. He was worthy to keep the ark of the covenant in his home for three months when David was moving it to Jerusalem. "The Ark of the Lord remained in Obed-Edom's house for three months, and the Lord blessed him and his household" (2 Samuel 6:11).

CHAPTER 22

Revelation 22:1–21

The Lord said, "Man has become like us, knowing good and evil. He must not eat from the Tree of Life and live forever." So God banished them from the Garden of Eden.

—Genesis 3:22–23

REVELATION 22:1–7. The angel points out the crystal clear River of the Water of Life flowing from the Throne of God and the Lamb. The River flows down the center of the street, and the Tree of Life is on both sides of the River. The Tree of Life continually produces fruit, and the leaves heal the nations. The curse is gone. The Throne of God and the Lamb is in the city, and They will rule forever. His servants see the face of God and they worship Him. His name is written on their foreheads. There is no night, and there is no need for the sun or lamps because The Lord God is the Light. God has sent His angel to show us these things. "I AM coming soon. Blessed are those who keep what is written on the scroll."

Adam and Eve were innocent! They didn't know good and evil! But they met evil in the form of a serpent who disputed God, and they took it upon themselves to try it out. The rest is all of history.

Is there only one throne? Jesus Himself told us that God the Father gave Him the right to judge. Now we know Who is sitting in the judgment seat.

> The Father judges no one. He has entrusted all judgment to the Son, so that all will honor the Son as they honor the Father. Anyone who does not honor the Son does not honor the Father who sent Him. (John 5:22–23)

When Adam and Eve listened to Satan as he disputed God's warning not to eat from the tree of knowledge of good and evil, and they disobeyed God (Genesis 2:16–17), they were banished from the garden of Eden, but it seems another tree, the tree of life, was the real reason Adam and Eve were banished from Eden (Genesis 3:22–23).

Now we see Eden regained. The curse has been lifted! God can now let us back into the garden of Eden. We can live forever! The rebellion and the evil have now been purged, and God can again fellowship with His friends face to face. God made us in His image because He wanted to interact with us and to fellowship with us. And He gave us the freedom of choice so that we could choose to fellowship with Him. Those in heaven are the ones who did choose to fellowship with Him.

Notice, we are made in the image of God. We look like Him, minus God's glory.

> God said, "Let us make man in Our image, to rule over the creatures and all the Earth, so God created man in His own image. (Genesis 1:26–27)

When Jesus came the first time, two thousand years ago, He did not come in our image. He came looking like Himself, minus the glory. Without His glory, Mary was able to carry Him for nine months and to deliver Him as the baby Jesus. He was able to grow from childhood and become a man, but He was in His own image. We are in His image. When we get to heaven, we will still be recognizable but better. Without our sin, we can see God face-to-face.

Jesus grew up in Nazareth, and apparently the family went to the synagogue on Saturday. Apparently, Jesus was a regular participant until He began His ministry.

Jesus returned to his hometown Nazareth and, as usual, He went to the synagogue on the Sabbath day. They handed the scroll of the prophet Isaiah to Jesus to read. Jesus unrolled the scroll and found and read this prophecy: "The Spirit of the Lord is on Me. He has anointed Me to preach good news to the poor, To proclaim freedom for the captives and prisoners and oppressed, to heal the blind. And to proclaim the Year of the Lord's favor" (Isaiah 61:1–2).

> Then He rolled up the scroll and sat down to teach. "Today this scripture is fulfilled." (Luke 4:14–21)

God has been telling us about His plan for our salvation ever since we sinned. True to His Word, Christ did come willingly to submit Himself as our Perfect Sacrifice. And now we are seeing "the rest of the story."

> REVELATION 22:8–20. I, John, saw and heard all of this. I fell down to worship the angel, but the angel cautioned me, "Don't do that. Just like you and those who heed this book, I am a servant of Jesus. Worship God. Do not seal up what you have written, because fulfillment is near. When that time comes, those who sin will sin more, the evil will be more evil, the good will be better, and the holy will still be holy. Jesus says, 'I have sent my angel to give you this message to the Churches. I Am coming soon. I Am the Alpha and the Omega, the Root and the Offspring of David, and the Morning Star. Those who wash their robes will be blessed forever and will have the right to enter the City and eat from the Tree of Life. Those who have strayed from God—the

immoral, idolaters, murderers, sorcerers, and liars—are banished. The Holy Spirit and the Bride call you to come. Anyone who is thirsty come and drink the Water of Life. Do not add to or take away from this Book. I Am coming quickly."

For the second time, John tried to worship the angel (Revelation 19:10). He is emphatically told to "Worship God!" Can you imagine how overcome John is by this great vision? This prophecy was not sealed; however, great periods of time had to elapse before some of it could be understood. The return of the children of Israel to the land only began to occur some seventy years ago. The formation of the European Union only came about some thirty years ago. Jesus said He would come soon, quickly, suddenly, swiftly!

In all this revelation we forget that Jesus initially addressed the churches. Now Jesus reminds us, the church, that the Great I Am is coming back.

John closes the book with a benediction:

REVELATION 22:21. The grace of our Lord Jesus Christ be with His people. Amen! Come, Lord Jesus!

All your people will be righteous; they will possess the land forever.

They are the shoot I planted with My hands for display of My splendor.

The least will be a thousand; the smallest a great Nation.

I Am the Lord…When the time comes, I will do this swiftly. (Isaiah 60:21–22)

ABOUT THE AUTHOR

 A. Elaine Williams Hart is a true Southerner, born in Monroe, Louisiana. She said, "It gets too cold here for me," so she moved further south to Baton Rouge and then spent a few years in New Orleans. She has two daughters who take care of her— bless them!

She is a retired attorney, holding a BS degree from Louisiana State University and a JD degree from Loyola University, New Orleans. Her employment has carried her from the sublime to the absurd. The sublime was good, but she loved the absurd!

Elaine taught Sunday school for many years and felt a need to actually teach the Bible, so she has studied and researched and has taught most of the Bible—a wonderful blessing! She wants everyone to join her in wanting to know what God *really* said.

CPSIA information can be obtained
at www.ICGtesting.com
Printed in the USA
BVHW080603300321
603653BV00005B/859